T0333372

365
POEMS
FOR
LIFE

Also by Allie Esiri
and available from Macmillan Children's Books:

A Nursery Rhyme for Every Night of the Year

A Poem for Every Autumn Day

A Poem for Every Day of the Year

A Poem for Every Night of the Year

A Poem for Every Spring Day

A Poem for Every Summer Day

A Poem for Every Winter Day

A Poet for Every Day of the Year

Shakespeare for Every Day of the Year

bluebird
books for life

365 POEMS FOR LIFE

An uplifting collection for
every day of the year

COMPILED BY

ALLIE ESIRI

First published 2023 by Bluebird
an imprint of Pan Macmillan
The Smithson, 6 Briset Street, London EC1M 5NR
EU representative: Macmillan Publishers Ireland Ltd, 1st Floor,
The Liffey Trust Centre, 117–126 Sheriff Street Upper,
Dublin 1, D01 YC43
Associated companies throughout the world
www.panmacmillan.com

ISBN 978-1-5290-8839-7

5 7 9 8 6

A CIP catalogue record for this book is available from the British Library.

Typeset by Palimpsest Book Production Ltd, Falkirk, Stirlingshire
Printed and bound by CPI Group (UK) Ltd, Croydon, CR0 4YY

Visit **www.panmacmillan.com/bluebird** to read more about all our books
and to buy them. You will also find features, author interviews and
news of any author events, and you can sign up for e-newsletters
so that you're always first to hear about our new releases.

For Serena, Susannah and Edward.

Contents

January
Beginnings

February
Love

March
Humour & Hope

April
Nature & Meditation

May
Gratitude

June
Joy

July
Escape

August
Friends & Family

September
Inspiration

October
Contemplation

November
Endings

December
Celebrations

January

Beginnings

JANUARY marks the ending of an old year and the beginning of a new one. The month is fittingly named after the Roman god of doorways, Janus. Described as the master of time and depicted with two heads, Janus simultaneously faces the past and the future, presiding over all types of transition; Henry Wadsworth Longfellow imagines him counting, 'The years that through my portals come and go.' The New Year is the gift of a liminal moment; a chance to look back and grieve what we might have lost and reflect on how we have changed, as well as an opportunity to look forward and think afresh.

For many the New Year symbolises the promise of reinvention. It is the moment when 'the future appears / like a blank sheet of paper / a clean calendar', says Scotland's former Makar (poet laureate) Jackie Kay. It is a time when the 'day is fresh-washed and fair', to borrow the words of Amy Lowell. It has the potential to be daunting, because the possibilities are unlimited and the future indeterminate. We can create resolutions and begin again, whether that should take the form of worrying less, of slowing down, or of deciding to stop 'shoring up eroding / friendships', as the American poet and activist Marge Piercy resolves.

Yet the poems collected in this month, and the wisdom they contain, are not solely for the turn of the year but launch us on our daily adventures. From the writing of the Japanese samurai and haiku master Matsuo Bashō, prompting us to be present in our surroundings and find beauty in wintry weather, to the more recent words of the Pakistan-born, Glaswegian poet Imtiaz Dharker's insistence that 'Everyone has the right / to infiltrate a piece of paper', these poets remind us that we are constantly in flux, constantly becoming and creating ourselves. Beginnings are by no means restricted to January.

Indeed, marking the New Year at all offers a reminder that the passage of time and our customary measurement of it is largely illusory anyway. In the earliest days of Rome, the year was only ten months long because January and February, being the barren wintry months, had no relevance to the agricultural calendar and simply were not named. The year began in March and ended in December.

In England, 1 January only became New Year's Day in 1752, when the Gregorian calendar was adopted. Prior to this, the New Year began on 25 March with the beginning of spring – our tax year reset-ting at the start of April is a remnant of this. The changeover wrought glitches in time. The calendar affected every area of life – not only festivals, saints' days and birthdays, but also more mundane matters, such as wages, rents and military or prison releases. Because the change demanded skipping from 2 September to 14 September, many felt that eleven days had been 'robbed' from them, but the change went ahead.

Besides the relative novelty of celebrating the new year on 1 January in England is the fact that many other cultures mark the turn of the year at an entirely different time; there is the lunisolar Chinese New Year (often known as the Spring Festival as it marks the end of winter), Judaism's Rosh Hashanah (meaning literally 'head of the year'; usually around late September or early October), and the Persian Nowruz (which falls on the spring equinox). While each calendar system attempts to justify its own particular division of the cosmic movements, the multiplicity of calendar systems in itself highlights that each is relative (even days are up for grabs – in the Hebrew and Islamic calen-dars, they begin at sunset).

So, when really does the year begin? As said by Margaret Tait: 'I'm asking for the pleasure of feeling there is no answer. / It's magic.' If we can bring ourselves to embrace it, this ambiguity, this mystery, can be freeing.

Ultimately, you could read these New Year poems every day or indeed on any day you wish. To quote the American author and poet Susan Coolidge, 'Every morn is the world made new'. Whether 1 January or any other day of the year, with the dawning of every day comes the promise of beginning and new opportunity. As the great Irish poet Brendan Kennelly writes, the world 'insists that we forever begin'.

For last year's words belong to last
year's language
And next year's words
await another voice.

T.S. Eliot

❧ I Worried

Mary Oliver 1935–2009

I worried a lot. Will the garden grow, will the rivers
flow in the right direction, will the earth turn
as it was taught, and if not, how shall
I correct it?

Was I right, was I wrong, will I be forgiven,
can I do better?

Will I ever be able to sing, even the sparrows
can do it and I am, well,
hopeless.

Is my eyesight fading or am I just imagining it,
am I going to get rheumatism,
lockjaw, dementia?

Finally, I saw that worrying had come to nothing.
And gave it up. And took my old body
and went out into the morning,
and sang.

❧ This Is the Time to be Slow (*Excerpt from* For the Break-Up of a Relationship)

John O'Donohue 1956–2008

This is the time to be slow,
Lie low to the wall
Until the bitter weather passes.

Try, as best you can, not to let
The wire brush of doubt
Scrape from your heart
All sense of yourself
And your hesitant light.

If you remain generous,
Time will come good;
And you will find your feet
Again on fresh pastures of promise,
Where the air will be kind
And blushed with beginning.

❧ The birthday of the world

Marge Piercy 1936–

On the birthday of the world
I begin to contemplate
what I have done and left
undone, but this year
not so much rebuilding

of my perennially damaged
psyche, shoring up eroding
friendships, digging out
stumps of old resentments
that refuse to rot on their own.

No, this year I want to call
myself to task for what
I have done and not done
for peace. How much have
I dared in opposition?

How much have I put
on the line for freedom?
For mine and others?
As these freedoms are pared,
sliced and diced, where

have I spoken out? Who
have I tried to move? In
this holy season, I stand
self-convicted of sloth
in a time when lies choke

the mind and rhetoric
bends reason to slithering
choking pythons. Here
I stand before the gates
opening, the fire dazzling

my eyes, and as I approach
what judges me, I judge
myself. Give me weapons
of minute destruction. Let
my words turn into sparks.

ॐ Begin

Brendan Kennelly 1936–2021

Begin again to the summoning birds
to the sight of light at the window,
begin to the roar of morning traffic
all along Pembroke Road.
Every beginning is a promise
born in light and dying in dark
determination and exaltation of springtime
flowering the way to work.
Begin to the pageant of queuing girls
the arrogant loneliness of swans in the canal
bridges linking the past and future
old friends passing through with us still.
Begin to the loneliness that cannot end
since it perhaps is what makes us begin,
begin to wonder at unknown faces
at crying birds in the sudden rain
at branches stark in the willing sunlight
at seagulls foraging for bread
at couples sharing a sunny secret
alone together while making good.
Though we live in a world that dreams of ending
that always seems about to give in
something that will not acknowledge conclusion
insists that we forever begin.

❧ Morning

Billy Collins 1941–

Why do we bother with the rest of the day,
the swale of the afternoon,
the sudden dip into evening,

then night with his notorious perfumes,
his many-pointed stars?

This is the best—
throwing off the light covers,
feet on the cold floor,
and buzzing around the house on espresso—

maybe a splash of water on the face,
a palmful of vitamins—
but mostly buzzing around the house on espresso,

dictionary and atlas open on the rug,
the typewriter waiting for the key of the head,
a cello on the radio,

and, if necessary, the windows—
trees fifty, a hundred years old
out there,
heavy clouds on the way
and the lawn steaming like a horse
in the early morning.

❧ Promise

Jackie Kay 1961–

Remember, the time of year
when the future appears
like a blank sheet of paper
a clean calendar, a new chance.
On thick white snow

you vow fresh footprints
then watch them go
with the wind's hearty gust.
Fill your glass. Here's tae us. Promises
made to be broken, made to last.

🐝 Rain

Don Paterson 1963–

I love all films that start with rain:
rain, braiding a windowpane
or darkening a hung-out dress
or streaming down her upturned face;

one big thundering downpour
right through the empty script and score
before the act, before the blame,
before the lens pulls through the frame

to where the woman sits alone
beside a silent telephone
or the dress lies ruined on the grass
or the girl walks off the overpass,

and all things flow out from that source
along their fatal watercourse.
However bad or overlong
such a film can do no wrong,

so when his native twang shows through
or when the boom dips into view
or when her speech starts to betray
its adaptation from a play,

I think to when we opened cold
on a starlit gutter, running gold
with the neon of a drugstore sign
and I'd read into its blazing line:

forget the ink, the milk, the blood —
all was washed clean with the flood
we rose up from the falling waters
the fallen rain's own sons and daughters

and none of this, none of this matters.

❧ Litmus

Margaret Tait 1918–1999

I don't know why it is that acid turns blue litmus pink,
And don't tell me you know
Because I'm sure you don't
—'Because it's acid.'—
That's no reason.
Acid is pink?
Nonsense.
With other reagents the pink's on the other side.
Why pink?
Why blue?
Why change?
And why change only in colour?
I'm not asking to get an answer and an explanation
About the negative logarithm of the concentration of
    free hydrogen ions;
I'm asking for the pleasure of feeling there is no
    answer.
It's magic.

❧ New Every Morning

Susan Coolidge 1835–1905

Every morn is the world made new.
You who are weary of sorrow and sinning,
Here is a beautiful hope for you, –
A hope for me and a hope for you.

All the past things are past and over;
The tasks are done and the tears are shed.
Yesterday's errors let yesterday cover;
Yesterday's wounds, which smarted and bled,
Are healed with the healing which night has shed.

Yesterday now is a part of forever,
Bound up in a sheaf, which God holds tight,
With glad days, and sad days, and bad days, which never
Shall visit us more with their bloom and their blight,
Their fulness of sunshine or sorrowful night.

Let them go, since we cannot re-live them,
Cannot undo and cannot atone;
God in his mercy receive, forgive them!
Only the new days are our own;
To-day is ours, and to-day alone.

Here are the skies all burnished brightly,
Here is the spent earth all re-born,
Here are the tired limbs springing lightly
To face the sun and to share with the morn
In the chrism of dew and the cool of dawn.

Every day is a fresh beginning;
Listen, my soul, to the glad refrain,
And, spite of old sorrow and older sinning,
And puzzles forecasted and possible pain,
Take heart with the day, and begin again.

❧ Up in the Morning Early

Robert Burns 1759–1796

Cauld blaws the wind frae east to west,
The drift is driving sairly;
Sae loud and shrill's I hear the blast,
I'm sure it's winter fairly.

Up in the morning's no for me,
Up in the morning early;
When a' the hills are cover'd wi' snaw,
I'm sure it's winter fairly.

The birds sit chittering in the thorn,
A' day they fare but sparely;
And lang's the night frae e'en to morn,
I'm sure it's winter fairly.

Up in the morning's no for me,
Up in the morning early;
When a' the hills are cover'd wi' snaw,
I'm sure it's winter fairly.

❧ 'Tis the First Snow

Matsuo Bashō 1644–1694
Translated by Robert Hass

'Tis the first snow—
Just enough to bend
The gladiolus leaves!

❧ Dawn

Helen Hunt Jackson 1830–1885

With a ring of silver,
    And a ring of gold,
   And a red, red rose
     Which illumines her face,
The sun, like a lover
  Who glows and is bold,
Wooes the lovely earth
   To his strong embrace.

🐦 Lines Composed in a Wood on a Windy Day

Anne Brontë 1820–1849

My soul is awakened, my spirit is soaring
  And carried aloft on the winds of the breeze;
For above and around me the wild wind is roaring,
  Arousing to rapture the earth and the seas.

The long withered grass in the sunshine is glancing,
  The bare trees are tossing their branches on high;
The dead leaves beneath them are merrily dancing,
  The white clouds are scudding across the blue sky.

I wish I could see how the ocean is lashing
  The foam of its billows to whirlwinds of spray;
I wish I could see how its proud waves are dashing,
  And hear the wild roar of their thunder to-day!

❧ January (from *The Poet's Calendar*)

Henry Wadsworth Longfellow 1807–1882

Janus am I; oldest of potentates;
    Forward I look, and backward, and below
I count, as god of avenues and gates,
    The years that through my portals come and go.

I block the roads, and drift the fields with snow;
    I chase the wild-fowl from the frozen fen;
My frosts congeal the rivers in their flow,
    My fires light up the hearths and hearts of men.

❧ When I Rise Up

Georgia Douglas Johnson 1880–1966

When I rise up above the earth,
And look down on the things that fetter me,
I beat my wings upon the air,
Or tranquil lie,
Surge after surge of potent strength
Like incense comes to me
When I rise up above the earth
And look down upon the things that fetter me.

❧ Bath

Amy Lowell 1874–1925

The day is fresh-washed and fair, and there is a smell of tulips and narcissus in the air.

The sunshine pours in at the bath-room window and bores through the water in the bath-tub in lathes and planes of greenish-white. It cleaves the water into flaws like a jewel, and cracks it to bright light.

Little spots of sunshine lie on the surface of the water and dance, dance, and their reflections wobble deliciously over the ceiling; a stir of my finger sets them whirring, reeling. I move a foot and the planes of light in the water jar. I lie back and laugh, and let the green-white water, the sun-flawed beryl water, flow over me. The day is almost too bright to bear, the green water covers me from the too bright day. I will lie here awhile and play with the water and the sun spots. The sky is blue and high. A crow flaps by the window, and there is a whiff of tulips and narcissus in the air.

❧ A Birthday

Christina Rossetti 1830–1894

My heart is like a singing bird
    Whose nest is in a water'd shoot;
My heart is like an apple-tree
    Whose boughs are bent with thickset fruit;
My heart is like a rainbow shell
    That paddles in a halcyon sea;
My heart is gladder than all these
    Because my love is come to me.

Raise me a dais of silk and down;
    Hang it with vair and purple dyes;
Carve it in doves and pomegranates,
    And peacocks with a hundred eyes;
Work it in gold and silver grapes,
    In leaves and silver fleurs-de-lys;
Because the birthday of my life
    Is come, my love is come to me.

ॐ The Blackbird of Spitalfields

Matthew Hollis 1971–

Four a.m. undone. No lock-ins, no vans
about their rounds, no running gangs,
just phrase on phrase of traffic heading north,
and up above the maze of roofs, a blackbird's flute,
unable to distinguish night from day.
Is it light or land that has him sing
or fuss for unreached company? And still,
for all his thirds and major fifths,
his song not song, but simple call and speech.
Nothing sings together on this earth but us.

?» Minority

Imtiaz Dharker 1954–

I was born a foreigner.
I carried on from there
to become a foreigner everywhere
I went, even in the place
planted with my relatives,
six-foot tubers sprouting roots,
their fingers and faces pushing up
new shoots of maize and sugar cane.

All kinds of places and groups
of people who have an admirable
history would, almost certainly,
distance themselves from me.

I don't fit,
like a clumsily translated poem;

like food cooked in milk of coconut
where you expected ghee or cream,
the unexpected aftertaste
of cardamom or neem.

There's always that point where
the language flips
into an unfamiliar taste;
where words tumble over
a cunning tripwire on the tongue;
where the frame slips,
the reception of an image
not quite tuned, ghost-outlined,
that signals, in their midst,
an alien.

And so I scratch, scratch
through the night, at this
growing scab on black and white.
Everyone has the right
to infiltrate a piece of paper.
A page doesn't fight back.

And, who knows, these lines
may scratch their way
into your head –
through all the chatter of community,
family, clattering spoons,
children being fed –
immigrate into your bed,
squat in your home,
and in a corner, eat your bread,

until, one day, you meet
the stranger sliding down your street,
realise you know the face
simplified to bone,
look into its outcast eyes
and recognise it as your own.

ꙮ The Present

Michael Donaghy 1954–2004

For the present there is just one moon,
though every level pond gives back another.

But the bright disc shining in the black lagoon,
perceived by astrophysicist and lover,

is milliseconds old. And even that light's
seven minutes older than its source.

And the stars we think we see on moonless nights
are long extinguished. And, of course,

this very moment, as you read this line,
is literally gone before you know it.

Forget the here-and-now. We have no time
but this device of wantonness and wit.

Make me this present then: your hand in mine,
and we'll live out our lives in it.

❧ Bright Star

John Keats 1795–1821

Bright star! would I were steadfast as thou art—
   Not in lone splendour hung aloft the night,
And watching, with eternal lids apart,
   Like Nature's patient sleepless Eremite,
The moving waters at their priestlike task
   Of pure ablution round earth's human shores,
Or gazing on the new soft fallen mask
   Of snow upon the mountains and the moors—
No—yet still steadfast, still unchangeable,
   Pillow'd upon my fair love's ripening breast,
To feel for ever its soft fall and swell,
   Awake for ever in a sweet unrest,
Still, still to hear her tender-taken breath,
And so live ever—or else swoon to death.

❧ The Good-Morrow

John Donne 1572–1631

I wonder, by my troth, what thou and I
Did, till we loved? Were we not weaned till then?
But sucked on country pleasures, childishly?
Or snorted we in the Seven Sleepers' den?
'Twas so; but this, all pleasures fancies be.
If ever any beauty I did see,
Which I desired, and got, 'twas but a dream of thee.

And now good-morrow to our waking souls,
Which watch not one another out of fear;
For love, all love of other sights controls,
And makes one little room an everywhere.
Let sea-discoverers to new worlds have gone,
Let maps to other, worlds on worlds have shown,
Let us possess one world, each hath one, and is one.

My face in thine eye, thine in mine appears,
And true plain hearts do in the faces rest;
Where can we find two better hemispheres,
Without sharp north, without declining west?
Whatever dies, was not mixed equally;
If our two loves be one, or, thou and I
Love so alike, that none do slacken, none can die.

❧ The Beginning

Rupert Brooke 1887–1915

Some day I shall rise and leave my friends
And seek you again through the world's far ends,
You whom I found so fair
(Touch of your hands and smell of your hair!),
My only god in the days that were.
My eager feet shall find you again,
Though the sullen years and the mark of pain
Have changed you wholly; for I shall know
(How could I forget having loved you so?),
In the sad half-light of evening,
The face that was all my sunrising.
So then at the ends of the earth I'll stand
And hold you fiercely by either hand,
And seeing your age and ashen hair
I'll curse the thing that once you were,
Because it is changed and pale and old
(Lips that were scarlet, hair that was gold!),
And I loved you before you were old and wise,
When the flame of youth was strong in your eyes,
— And my heart is sick with memories.

❧ Little Gidding (from *Four Quartets*)

T.S. Eliot 1888–1965

I am not eager to rehearse
My thoughts and theory which you have forgotten.
These things have served their purpose: let them be.
So with your own, and pray they be forgiven
By others, as I pray you to forgive
Both bad and good. Last season's fruit is eaten
And the fullfed beast shall kick the empty pail.
For last year's words belong to last year's language
And next year's words await another voice.

❧ In The Beginning

Dylan Thomas 1914–1953

In the beginning was the three-pointed star,
One smile of light across the empty face;
One bough of bone across the rooting air,
The substance forked that marrowed the first sun;
And, burning cyphers on the round of space,
Heaven and hell mixed as they spun.

In the beginning was the pale signature,
Three-syllabled and starry as the smile;
And after came the imprints on the water,
Stamp of the minted face upon the moon;
The blood that touched the crosstree and the grail
Touched the first cloud and left a sign.

In the beginning was the mounting fire
That set alight the weathers from a spark,
A three-eyed, red-eyed spark, blunt as a flower;
Life rose and spouted from the rolling seas,
Burst in the roots, pumped from the earth and rock
The secret oils that drive the grass.

In the beginning was the word, the word
That from the solid bases of the light
Abstracted all the letters of the void;
And from the cloudy bases of the breath
The word flowed up, translating to the heart
First characters of birth and death.

In the beginning was the secret brain.
The brain was celled and soldered in the thought
Before the pitch was forking to a sun;
Before the veins were shaking in their sieve,
Blood shot and scattered to the winds of light
The ribbed original of love.

❧ Genesis

Geoffrey Hill 1932–2016

I

Against the burly air I strode,
Where the tight ocean heaves its load,
Crying the miracles of God.

And first I brought the sea to bear
Upon the dead weight of the land;
And the waves flourished at my prayer,
The rivers spawned their sand.

And where the streams were salt and full,
The tough pig-headed salmon strove,
Curbing the ebb and the tide's pull
To reach the steady hills above.

II

The second day I stood and saw
The osprey plunge with triggered claw,
Feathering blood along the shore,
To lay the living sinew bare.

III

And I renounced, on the fourth day,
This fierce and unregenerate clay,

Building as a huge myth for man
The watery Leviathan,

And made the glove-winged albatross
Scour the ashes of the sea
Where Capricorn and Zero cross,
A brooding immortality—
Such as the charméd phoenix has
In the unwithering tree.

IV
The phoenix burns as cold as frost;
And, like a legendary ghost
The phantom-bird goes wild and lost,
Upon pointless ocean tossed.

So, the fifth day, I turned again
To flesh and blood and the blood's pain.

V
On the sixth day, as I rode
In haste about the works of God,
With spurs I plucked the horse's blood.

By blood we live, the hot, the cold
To ravage and redeem the world:
There is no bloodless myth will hold.

And by Christ's blood are men made free
Though in close shrouds their bodies lie
Under the rough pelt of the sea;

Though Earth has rolled beneath her weight
The bones that cannot bear the light.

❧ The Seedling

Paul Laurence Dunbar 1872–1906

As a quiet little seedling
    Lay within its darksome bed,
To itself it fell a-talking,
    And this is what it said:

"I am not so very robust,
    But I'll do the best I can;"
And the seedling from that moment
    Its work of life began.

So it pushed a little leaflet
    Up into the light of day,
To examine the surroundings
    And show the rest the way.

The leaflet liked the prospect,
    So it called its brother, Stem;
Then two other leaflets heard it,
    And quickly followed them.

To be sure, the haste and hurry
    Made the seedling sweat and pant;
But almost before it knew it
    It found itself a plant.

The sunshine poured upon it,
    And the clouds they gave a shower;
And the little plant kept growing
    Till it found itself a flower.

Little folks, be like the seedling,
    Always do the best you can;
Every child must share life's labor
    Just as well as every man.

And the sun and showers will help you
    Through the lonesome, struggling hours,
Till you raise to light and beauty
    Virtue's fair, unfading flowers.

Velvet Shoes

Elinor Wylie 1885–1928

Let us walk in the white snow
  In a soundless space;
With footsteps quiet and slow,
  At a tranquil pace,
  Under veils of white lace.

I shall go shod in silk,
  And you in wool,
White as a white cow's milk,
  More beautiful
  Than the breast of a gull.

We shall walk through the still town
  In a windless peace;
We shall step upon white down,
  Upon silver fleece,
  Upon softer than these.

We shall walk in velvet shoes;
  Wherever we go
Silence will fall like dews
  On white silence below.
  We shall walk in the snow.

❧ The Snow Man

Wallace Stevens 1879–1955

One must have a mind of winter
To regard the frost and the boughs
Of the pine-trees crusted with snow;

And have been cold a long time
To behold the junipers shagged with ice,
The spruces rough in the distant glitter

Of the January sun; and not to think
Of any misery in the sound of the wind,
In the sound of a few leaves,

Which is the sound of the land
Full of the same wind
That is blowing in the same bare place

For the listener, who listens in the snow,
And, nothing himself, beholds
Nothing that is not there and the nothing that is.

❧ I started Early – Took my Dog –

Emily Dickinson 1830–1886

I started Early – Took my Dog –
And visited the Sea –
The Mermaids in the Basement
Came out to look at me –

And Frigates – in the Upper Floor
Extended Hempen Hands –
Presuming Me to be a Mouse –
Aground – opon the Sands –

But no Man moved Me – till the Tide
Went past my simple Shoe –
And past my Apron – and my Belt
And past my Boddice – too –

And made as He would eat me up –
As wholly as a Dew
Opon a Dandelion's Sleeve –
And then – I started – too –

And He – He followed – close behind –
I felt His Silver Heel
Opon my Ancle – Then My Shoes
Would overflow with Pearl –

Until We met the Solid Town –
No One He seemed to know –
And bowing – with a Mighty look –
At me – The Sea withdrew –

❧ The New Colossus

Emma Lazarus 1849–1887

Not like the brazen giant of Greek fame,
With conquering limbs astride from land to land;
Here at our sea-washed, sunset gates shall stand
A mighty woman with a torch, whose flame
Is the imprisoned lightning, and her name
Mother of Exiles. From her beacon-hand
Glows world-wide welcome; her mild eyes command
The air-bridged harbor that twin cities frame.
"Keep, ancient lands, your storied pomp!" cries she
With silent lips. "Give me your tired, your poor,
Your huddled masses yearning to breathe free,
The wretched refuse of your teeming shore.
Send these, the homeless, tempest-tost to me,
I lift my lamp beside the golden door!"

February

Love

F EBRUARY is the month of love, or so they say. But what is love? As the great Anglo-American poet W.H. Auden asks, in one of his lighter moods, 'Is it prickly to touch as a hedge is, / Or soft as eiderdown fluff? / Is it sharp or quite smooth at the edges? / O tell me the truth about love.'

Elizabeth Barrett Browning's sonnet also begins with a question, opening with the line: 'How do I love thee? Let me count the ways.' Many languages have multiple different words to express the infinitely varied concepts that in English are all denoted 'love'. The Ancient Greeks, for example, philosophised four main categories of love; friendly (*philia*), familial (*storge*), unconditional (*agape*) and, finally, romantic (*eros*) – that whimsical, wonderful, and infinitely varied type of love to which we devote February.

But in English, with such a poverty of words to describe the feeling, love's diversity requires a loosening of the tongue, as with the former Poet Laureate Carol Ann Duffy's 'impossible song', 'Words, Wide Night', 'This is pleasurable. Or shall I cross that out and say / it is sad? In one of the tenses I singing / an impossible song of desire that you cannot hear.' Otherwise, poets are able to loosen language by playing with the page itself, as in E.E. Cummings' work. Simple descriptions do not suffice: for as Neil Gaiman writes, 'It's not the kisses, or never just the kisses: it's what they mean.'

And the tradition of celebrating love in February may be more complex than the popular Valentine's Day legends would have us believe. For hundreds of years before it became the holiday of love, St. Valentine's Day was celebrated as a Christian feast day for one of many men martyred by the Romans.

The first recorded connection between Valentine's Day and love appears in the medieval poet Chaucer's dream poem 'The Parliament of Fowls' (1382), written to commemorate the first anniversary of the young King Richard II's engagement to Anne of Bohemia. The work (which is not in this collection) is a sweet legend in which all birds gather to choose their mate: 'For this was on seynt Valentynes day / Whan every foul cometh ther to chese his make' ('For this was on St. Valentine's Day, / When every fowl comes there to choose his match'). The lovebirds of early spring and the pairing off of young lovers have been associated ever since.

Shortly after Chaucer's poem dates the earliest description we have of 14 February as a love celebration; Charles VI of France, in 1400, organized festivities for his Court of Love, including poetry competitions, jousting and dancing. Two hundred years later, Valentine's Day's association with love was well-established enough for it to be referenced mournfully by Ophelia in Shakespeare's *Hamlet* (1601).

Whether love is conjugal, unrequited, hidden, forbidden, comic, improbable, old or young, there is a poem to guide us through its whimsical ways and infinite variety. U.A. Fanthorpe's 'Atlas' reminds us to appreciate the things that we may have grown used to, with its opening, 'There is a kind of love called maintenance, / Which stores the WD40 and knows when to use it,' while John Osborne's tale about an old couple, once young, reminds us to take risks: 'Their third date was a pub Sunday roast, / walking her back home he proposed.' Love can take the form of Fleur Adcock's euphemistic 'jump-starting' and Emily Dickinson's ecstatic 'Wild Nights!' But it can equally be Simon Armitage's dead arm, or, in Wendy Cope's work, make itself known when 'the juke-box inside me is playing a song'.

The poets are able to capture and express the vulnerability we experience in love, from W.B. Yeats' plea to his lover, 'Tread softly because you tread on my dreams' to Derek Walcott's promise to a lover at the end of a relationship that 'You will love again the stranger who was your self'.

this is the wonder that's
keeping the stars apart
i carry your heart(i carry it in my heart)

E.E. Cummings

❧ First Love

John Clare 1793–1864

I ne'er was struck before that hour
   With love so sudden and so sweet,
Her face it bloomed like a sweet flower
   And stole my heart away complete.
My face turned pale as deadly pale,
   My legs refused to walk away,
And when she looked, what could I ail?
   My life and all seemed turned to clay.

And then my blood rushed to my face
   And took my eyesight quite away,
The trees and bushes round the place
   Seemed midnight at noonday.
I could not see a single thing,
   Words from my eyes did start—
They spoke as chords do from the string,
   And blood burnt round my heart.

Are flowers the winter's choice?
   Is love's bed always snow?
She seemed to hear my silent voice,
   Not love's appeals to know.
I never saw so sweet a face
   As that I stood before.
My heart has left its dwelling-place
   And can return no more.

❧ O Tell me the Truth About Love

W.H. Auden 1907–1973

Some say love's a little boy,
   And some say it's a bird,
Some say it makes the world go round,
   And some say that's absurd,
And when I asked the man next door,
   Who looked as if he knew,
His wife got very cross indeed,
   And said it wouldn't do.

Does it look like a pair of pyjamas,
   Or the ham in a temperance hotel?
Does its odour remind one of llamas,
   Or has it a comforting smell?
Is it prickly to touch as a hedge is,
   Or soft as eiderdown fluff?
Is it sharp or quite smooth at the edges?
   O tell me the truth about love.

Our history books refer to it
   In cryptic little notes,
It's quite a common topic on
   The Transatlantic boats;
I've found the subject mentioned in
   Accounts of suicides,
And even seen it scribbled on
   The backs of railway guides.

Does it howl like a hungry Alsatian,
  Or boom like a military band?
Could one give a first-rate imitation
  On a saw or a Steinway Grand?
Is its singing at parties a riot?
  Does it only like Classical stuff?
Will it stop when one wants to be quiet?
  O tell me the truth about love.

I looked inside the summer-house;
  It wasn't ever there;
I tried the Thames at Maidenhead,
  And Brighton's bracing air,
I don't know what the blackbird sang,
  Or what the tulip said;
But it wasn't in the chicken-run,
  Or underneath the bed.

Can it pull extraordinary faces?
  Is it usually sick on a swing?
Does it spend all its time at the races,
  Or fiddling with pieces of string?
Has it views of its own about money?
  Does it think Patriotism enough?
Are its stories vulgar but funny?
  O tell me the truth about love.

When it comes, will it come without warning,
    Just as I'm picking my nose?
Will it knock on my door in the morning,
    Or tread in the bus on my toes?
Will it come like a change in the weather?
    Will its greeting be courteous or rough?
Will it alter my life altogether?
    O tell me the truth about love.

❧ Love at First Sight

Robert Graves 1895–1985

'Love at first sight,' some say, misnaming
Discovery of twinned helplessness
Against the huge tug of procreation.

But friendship at first sight? This also
Catches fiercely at the surprised heart
So that the cheek blanches and then blushes.

❧ After the Lunch

Wendy Cope 1945–

On Waterloo Bridge, where we said our goodbyes,
The weather conditions bring tears to my eyes.
I wipe them away with a black woolly glove
And try not to notice I've fallen in love.

On Waterloo Bridge I am trying to think:
This is nothing. You're high on the charm and the drink.
But the juke-box inside me is playing a song
That says something different. And when was it wrong?

On Waterloo Bridge with the wind in my hair
I am tempted to skip. *You're a fool.* I don't care.
The head does its best but the heart is the boss –
I admit it before I am halfway across.

?❧ Conviction (IV)

Stevie Smith 1902–1971

I like to get off with people,
I like to lie in their arms
I like to be held and lightly kissed,
Safe from all alarms.

I like to laugh and be happy
With a beautiful kiss,
I tell you, in all the world
There is no bliss like this.

❦ Down the pub

Kae Tempest 1985–

It was something about the shape of his face
the size of him. I couldn't take my eyes off him.

I just wanted him to know without me saying
that I needed him to put me in my place.

We were joking, all together, shooting pool.
I was standing, legs apart, smoking fags and swearing.

Beside me, with their slender waists and shipwreck eyes
the girls were dancing, and I was dying

To be like them; until one put her breasts
against my body and my feelings changed.

❧ may i feel said he

E.E. Cummings 1894–1962

may i feel said he
(i'll squeal said she
just once said he)
it's fun said she

(may i touch said he
how much said she
a lot said he)
why not said she

(let's go said he
not too far said she
what's too far said he
where you are said she)

may i stay said he
which way said she
like this said he
if you kiss said she

may i move said he
is it love said she)
if you're willing said he
(but you're killing said she

but it's life said he
but your wife said she
now said he)
ow said she

(tiptop said he
don't stop said she
oh no said he)
go slow said she

(cccome?said he
ummm said she)
you're divine!said he
(you are Mine said she)

❧ Wild Nights!

Emily Dickinson 1830–1886

Wild nights – Wild nights!
Were I with thee
Wild nights should be
Our luxury!

Futile – the winds –
To a Heart in port –
Done with the Compass –
Done with the Chart!

Rowing in Eden –
Ah – the Sea!
Might I but moor – tonight –
In thee!

❧ Coupling

Fleur Adcock 1934–

On the wall above the bedside lamp
A large crane-fly is jump-starting
A smaller crane-fly – or vice versa.
They do it tail to tail, like Volkswagens:
Their engines must be in their rears.

It looks easy enough. Let's try it.

❧ Let me put it this way

Simon Armitage 1963–

Let me put it this way:
if you came to lay

your sleeping head
against my arm or sleeve,

and if my arm went dead,
or if I had to take my leave

at midnight, I should rather
cleave it from the joint or seam

than make a scene
or bring you round.

There,
how does that sound?

❧ Close, Close All Night

Elizabeth Bishop 1911–1979

Close close all night
the lovers keep.
They turn together
in their sleep,

close as two pages
in a book
that read each other
in the dark.

Each knows all
the other knows,
learned by heart
from head to toes.

❧ He Wishes for the Cloths of Heaven

W.B. Yeats 1865–1939

Had I the heavens' embroidered cloths,
Enwrought with golden and silver light,
The blue and the dim and the dark cloths
Of night and light and the half light,
I would spread the cloths under your feet:
But I, being poor, have only my dreams;
I have spread my dreams under your feet;
Tread softly because you tread on my dreams.

❧ Valentine

Wendy Cope 1945–

My heart has made its mind up
And I'm afraid it's you.
Whatever you've got lined up,
My heart has made its mind up
And if you can't be signed up
This year, next year will do.
My heart has made its mind up
And I'm afraid it's you.

❧ Valentine

John Fuller 1937–

The things about you I appreciate
May seem indelicate:
I'd like to find you in the shower
And chase the soap for half an hour.
I'd like to have you in my power
And see your eyes dilate.
I'd like to have your back to scour
And other parts to lubricate.
Sometimes I feel it is my fate
To chase you screaming up a tower
Or make you cower
By asking you to differentiate
Nietzsche from Schopenhauer.
I'd like successfully to guess your weight
And win you at a fête.
I'd like to offer you a flower.

I like the hair upon your shoulders,
Falling like water over boulders.
I like the shoulders too: they are essential.
Your collar-bones have great potential
(I'd like your particulars in folders
Marked Confidential).

I like your cheeks, I like your nose,
I like the way your lips disclose
The neat arrangement of your teeth
(Half above and half beneath)
In rows.

I like your eyes, I like their fringes.
The way they focus on me gives me twinges.
Your upper arms drive me berserk.
I like the way your elbows work.
On hinges . . .

I like your wrists, I like your glands,
I like the fingers on your hands.
I'd like to teach them how to count,
And certain things we might exchange,
Something familiar for something strange.
I'd like to give you just the right amount
And get some change.

I like it when you tilt your cheek up.
I like the way you not and hold a teacup.
I like your legs when you unwind them.
Even in trousers I don't mind them.
I like each softly-moulded kneecap.

I like the little crease behind them.
I'd always know, without a recap,
Where to find them.

I like the sculpture of your ears.
I like the way your profile disappears
Whenever you decide to turn and face me.
I'd like to cross two hemispheres
And have you chase me.
I'd like to smuggle you across frontiers
Or sail with you at night into Tangiers.
I'd like you to embrace me.

I'd like to see you ironing your skirt
And cancelling other dates.
I'd like to button up your shirt.
I like the way your chest inflates.
I'd like to soothe you when you're hurt
Or frightened senseless by invertebrates.

I'd like you even if you were malign
And had a yen for sudden homicide.
I'd let you put insecticide
Into my wine.
I'd even like you if you were Bride
Of Frankenstein
Or something ghoulish out of Mamoulian's
Jekyll and Hyde.
I'd even like you as my Julian
Or Norwich or Cathleen ni Houlihan.
How melodramatic
If you were something muttering in attics
Like Mrs Rochester or a student of Boolean
Mathematics.

You are the end of self-abuse.
You are the eternal feminine.
I'd like to find a good excuse
To call on you and find you in.
I'd like to put my hand beneath your chin,
And see you grin.
I'd like to taste your Charlotte Russe,
I'd like to feel my lips upon your skin
I'd like to make you reproduce.

I'd like you in my confidence.
I'd like to be your second look.
I'd like to let you try the French Defence
And mate you with my rook.
I'd like to be your preference
And hence
I'd like to be around when you unhook.
I'd like to be your only audience,
The final name in your appointment book,
Your future tense.

❧ Love after Love

Derek Walcott 1930–2017

The time will come
when, with elation
you will greet yourself arriving
at your own door, in your own mirror
and each will smile at the other's welcome,

and say, sit here. Eat.
You will love again the stranger who was your self.
Give wine. Give bread. Give back your heart
to itself, to the stranger who has loved you

all your life, whom you ignored
for another, who knows you by heart.
Take down the love letters from the bookshelf,

the photographs, the desperate notes,
peel your own image from the mirror.
Sit. Feast on your life.

❧ Dark Sonnet

Neil Gaiman 1960–

I don't think that I've been in love as such,
Although I liked a few folk pretty well.
Love must be vaster than my smiles or touch,
For brave men died and empires rose and fell
For love: girls followed boys to foreign lands
And men have followed women into Hell.

In plays and poems someone understands
There's something makes us more than blood and bone
And more than biological demands . . .
For me, love's like the wind, unseen, unknown.
I see the trees are bending where it's been,
I know that it leaves wreckage where it's blown.
I really don't know what "I love you" means.
I think it means "Don't leave me here alone."

❧ Wedding

Alice Oswald 1966–

From time to time our love is like a sail
and when the sail begins to alternate
from tack to tack, it's like a swallowtail
and when the swallow flies it's like a coat;
and if the coat is yours, it has a tear
like a wide mouth and when the mouth begins
to draw the wind, it's like a trumpeter
and when the trumpet blows, it blows like millions . . .
and this, my love, when millions come and go
beyond the need of us, is like a trick;
and when the trick begins, it's like a toe
tip-toeing on a rope, which is like luck;
and when the luck begins, it's like a wedding,
which is like love, which is like everything.

❧ i carry your heart with me (i carry it in

E.E. Cummings 1894–1962

i carry your heart with me(i carry it in
my heart)i am never without it(anywhere
i go you go,my dear;and whatever is done
by only me is your doing,my darling)
                                i fear
no fate(for you are my fate,my sweet)i want
no world(for beautiful you are my world,my true)
and it's you are whatever a moon has always meant
and whatever a sun will always sing is you

here is the deepest secret nobody knows
(here is the root of the root and the bud of the bud
and the sky of the sky of a tree called life;which grows
higher than soul can hope or mind can hide)
and this is the wonder that's keeping the stars apart

i carry your heart(i carry it in my heart)

❧ Scaffolding

Seamus Heaney 1939–2013

Masons, when they start upon a building,
Are careful to test out the scaffolding;

Make sure that planks won't slip at busy points,
Secure all ladders, tighten bolted joints.

And yet all this comes down when the job's done
Showing off walls of sure and solid stone.

So if, my dear, there sometimes seem to be
Old bridges breaking between you and me

Never fear. We may let the scaffolds fall
Confident that we have built our wall.

❧ Hinterhof

James Fenton 1949–

Stay near to me and I'll stay near to you—
As near as you are dear to me will do,
   Near as the rainbow to the rain,
   The west wind to the windowpane,
As fire to the hearth, as dawn to dew.

Stay true to me and I'll stay true to you—
As true as you are new to me will do,
   New as the rainbow in the spray,
   Utterly new in every way,
New in the way that what you say is true.

Stay near to me, stay true to me. I'll stay
As near, as true to you as heart could pray.
   Heart never hoped that one might be
   Half of the things you are to me—
The dawn, the fire, the rainbow and the day.

❧ The Vows

Michael Symmons Roberts 1963–

We pledge to wake each morning face-to-face,
to shun the orders of the busy sun,
we promise to disturb each other's peace.

And we will, yes, gaze at the pining moon,
will pick out brine-blown glass-gems from the strand,
will read our future scratched onto a stone.

We both believe that silence turns to sand
and promise not to add to the unsaid,
we meet here as the raging sea meets land.

We want the risen life before we're dead,
our passion will be squandered more than spent,
we hereby swear to spend our days in bed.

We're naked, till we wear each other's scent
and recognise it quicker than our own.
You start and finish me, you're my extent.

🐝 Wedding Thoughts: All I know about love

Neil Gaiman 1960–

This is everything I have to tell you about love: *nothing*.
This is everything I've learned about marriage: *nothing*.

Only that the world out there is complicated,
and there are beasts in the night, and delight and pain,
and the only thing that makes it okay, sometimes,
is to reach out a hand in the darkness and find another
    hand to squeeze,
and not to be alone.

It's not the kisses, or never just the kisses: it's what they
    mean.
Somebody's got your back.
Somebody knows your worst self and somehow doesn't
    want to rescue you
or send for the army to rescue them.

It's not two broken halves becoming one.
It's the light from a distant lighthouse bringing you both
    safely home
because home is wherever you are both together.

So this is everything I have to tell you about love and
    marriage: *nothing*,
like a book without pages or a forest without trees.

Because there are things you cannot know before you
  experience them.
Because no study can prepare you for the joys or the trials.
Because nobody else's love, nobody else's marriage, is like
  yours,
and it's a road you can only learn by walking it,
a dance you cannot be taught,
a song that did not exist before you began, together, to
  sing.

And because in the darkness you will reach out a hand,
not knowing for certain if someone else is even there.
And your hands will meet,
and then neither of you will ever need to be alone again.

And that's all I know about love.

੨ Atlas

U.A. Fanthorpe 1929–2009

There is a kind of love called maintenance,
Which stores the WD40 and knows when to use it;

Which checks the insurance, and doesn't forget
The milkman; which remembers to plant bulbs;

Which answers letters; which knows the way
The money goes; which deals with dentists

And Road Fund Tax and meeting trains,
And postcards to the lonely; which upholds

The permanently ricketty elaborate
Structures of living; which is Atlas.

And maintenance is the sensible side of love,
Which knows what time and weather are doing
To my brickwork; insulates my faulty wiring;
Laughs at my dryrotten jokes; remembers
My need for gloss and grouting; which keeps
My suspect edifice upright in the air,
As Atlas did the sky.

❧ How Do I Love Thee? (Sonnet 43)

Elizabeth Barrett Browning 1806–1861

How do I love thee? Let me count the ways.
I love thee to the depth and breadth and height
My soul can reach, when feeling out of sight
For the ends of being and ideal grace.
I love thee to the level of every day's
Most quiet need, by sun and candle-light.
I love thee freely, as men strive for right.
I love thee purely, as they turn from praise.
I love thee with the passion put to use
In my old griefs, and with my childhood's faith.
I love thee with a love I seemed to lose
With my lost saints. I love thee with the breath,
Smiles, tears, of all my life; and, if God choose,
I shall but love thee better after death.

❧ interior w/ ceiling fan

Kayo Chingonyi 1987–

wish that we could lie here
for the rest of our lives
the blades of the fan above us
whirling like a tanguera's skirt
everything outside this room
a distant country
let me be this unguarded always
speaking without need of words
because breath is the oldest language
any of us know

❧ Love

Hannah Lowe 1976–

Mornings, we'd find salmon bagels from Brick Lane,
Char siu buns and Soho flower rolls,
A box of Motichoor.

Upstairs, you huddled in the covers, curtains drawn,
The talk show murmur from the radio,
A stave of light across the wall.

❧ Words, Wide Night

Carol Ann Duffy 1955–

Somewhere on the other side of this wide night
and the distance between us, I am thinking of you.
The room is turning slowly away from the moon.

This is pleasurable. Or shall I cross that out and say
it is sad? In one of the tenses I singing
an impossible song of desire that you cannot hear.

La lala la. See? I close my eyes and imagine
the dark hills I would have to cross
to reach you. For I am in love with you and this

is what it is like or what it is like in words.

❧ To a Stranger

Walt Whitman 1819–1892

Passing stranger! you do not know how longingly I look
  upon you,
You must be he I was seeking, or she I was seeking, (it
  comes to me as of a dream,)
I have somewhere surely lived a life of joy with you,
All is recall'd as we flit by each other, fluid, affectionate,
  chaste, matured,
You grew up with me, were a boy with me or a girl with
  me,
I ate with you and slept with you, your body has become
  not yours only nor left my body mine only,
You give me the pleasure of your eyes, face, flesh, as we
  pass, you take of my beard, breast, hands, in return,
I am not to speak to you, I am to think of you when I sit
  alone or wake at night alone,
I am to wait, I do not doubt I am to meet you again,
I am to see to it that I do not lose you.

❧ There Is Handholding Still

John Osborne 1981–

My friend's grandparents married
three weeks after they first met.

Their third date was a pub Sunday roast,
walking her back home he proposed.

Two eighteen year olds saying
'I've got a good feeling about this.'

I think about them when I need reminding
sometimes we have to take risks.

March

Humour & Hope

W E turn to poets to help us express the complexity of being human; poets have invariably been able to articulate what the rest of us find to be ineffable. Poetry is the language that we reach for when everyday expressions fail us, and in the happiest and bleakest moments, great poems offer humour and hope.

As winter begins to thaw, the promise of spring brings a great source of hope. No poet better expresses this than the great Romantic Samuel Taylor Coleridge, describing that time when 'All Nature seems at work' and 'Winter, slumbering in the open air, / Wears on his smiling face a dream of Spring!' For many of the poets, birds are a great symbol of hope; for Emily Dickinson, it is a bird 'that perches in the soul' and never stops singing, if only we can bring ourselves to listen to its song. And Edward Thomas' poem 'Thaw' shows how poetry can encourage you to view life from the perspective of the 'speculating rooks', who are able to see, even when it is obscured from our human view. In 'Winter pass', Langston Hughes twists this trope, imagining hopeful dreams as the wings of our lives: 'if dreams die/ Life is a broken-winged bird/ That cannot fly.'

For other poets, different elements of nature provide hope. The eighteenth-century Japanese poet Yosa Buson's haiku emphasises that even our solitude on lonely nights can be improved if we choose to 'take the moon as a friend', while Ella Higginson reminds us to bear our trials patiently: 'If you work, if you wait, you will find the place / Where the four-leaf clovers grow.' There is hope to be found everywhere, if we can only cultivate the right mindset. Arthur Hugh Clough's seminal poem 'Say not the Struggle Nought Availeth' illuminates how even a cynical mindset can be twisted logically to offer reprieve: 'If hope were dupes, fears may be liars.'

Even in the bleakest of times poetry can touch your soul and elicit a smile, or offer the promise of hope. A marvellous example is Margaret Fishback's dry wit: '[When] I am wearing something new / And reassuring, I decide / It might be better to eschew / My tendency to cyanide'. The promise here and in so many of the poems collected for March is simply that even the blackest of moods and the darkest of circumstances are ultimately fickle – and by making you laugh, the poets prove the truth in such a message.

Poets, like stand-up comedians, can find comedy in the familiar and even the mundane with shrewd and unusual observations. After all, the poet's role, as Dickinson said, is to 'Tell all the truth, but tell it slant.' How else to interpret Maggie Smith's musing on trying to enthuse her children about a world that can be so unkind? Smith's emphasis on seeing the positives turns on the humour of the recognisable comparison of herself to an estate agent: 'Any decent realtor, / walking you through a real shithole, chirps on / about good bones: This place could be beautiful, / right? You could make this place beautiful.' And in Ian Duhig's 'Bridled Vows', candour is a source of humour with its attendant refusal to speak in superlative terms: 'I will be faithful to you, I do vow, / but not until the seas have all run dry / et cetera. Although I mean it now / I'm not a prophet and I will not lie.' The humour shatters the illusion of the 'perfect wife', before eventually coming to a candid conclusion of hope in the average relationship's potential: 'We might work out. No blame if we do not. / With all my heart, I think it's worth a shot.'

Comedy not only provides a source of hope or redirection in hard times, but encourages us to reconnect with one another. Poetry is descended from the oral tradition and so there is always pleasure in reading poems aloud, but in the case of comic poems they seem to insist on it, demanding to be shared. In general, poetry intensifies and this is especially the case with humour. Sometimes it achieves this through our anticipation of the rhymes, when you can hear the joke coming, as in another of Margaret Fishback's poems – the cryptically-titled 'Virtue is its Own Reward.' Otherwise, poets yoke words together, creating delightfully unusual combinations. Take, for instance, the 'Brief History of Modern Art in Poetry' by Brian Bilston, who is known, thanks to his pseudonym, as the Banksy of poetry. How else to explain his poetic explanation of Social Realism: 'Roses are dead. / Violence is rife./ Don't sugar coat/ This bitter life'?

So too does the brilliant Dorothy Parker's 'Symptom Recital' toy with our expectations. In the lines, 'I'm disillusioned, empty-breasted./ For what I think, I'd be arrested./ I am not sick, I am not well./ My quondam dreams are shot to hell', both the feminine rhyme on the sincerely-felt 'empty-breasted' and the exaggeration of 'I'd be arrested', and the disparity between the formal register of 'quondam' (meaning 'former') and the vernacular 'shot to hell' provide the comic turn. In both this poem and 'One Perfect Rose', with which the month commences, Parker proves the lie in the claim that Americans lack the dry, ironic humour attributed to the British; she elevated cynicism to an art form with her wit.

Yet it is interesting when reading poetry not to lose sight of the human; every poet has a unique and full life behind their work. Like so many of the greatest comedians, Dorothy Parker suffered from depression, while Emily Dickinson's struggles with melancholic anxiety underpin her hopeful poetry. The hope and humour conveyed in the poetry of this collection can be subtly intertwined with the poet's own need for the emotional reprieve that they offer – a reminder that we are never alone.

When I am sad and weary
When I think all hope has gone
When I walk along High Holborn
I think of you with nothing on

Adrian Mitchell

❧ Symptom Recital

Dorothy Parker 1893–1967

I do not like my state of mind;
I'm bitter, querulous, unkind.
I hate my legs, I hate my hands,
I do not yearn for lovelier lands.
I dread the dawn's recurrent light;
I hate to go to bed at night.
I snoot at simple, earnest folk.
I cannot take the gentlest joke.
I find no peace in paint or type.
My world is but a lot of tripe.
I'm disillusioned, empty-breasted.
For what I think, I'd be arrested.
I am not sick, I am not well.
My quondam dreams are shot to hell.
My soul is crushed, my spirit sore;
I do not like me any more.
I cavil, quarrel, grumble, grouse.
I ponder on the narrow house.
I shudder at the thought of men. . . .
I'm due to fall in love again.

❧ Virtue is its Own Reward

Margaret Fishback 1900–1985

I wish my frank and open face
Held just one tiny little trace
Of something that approaches guile.
I'd like an enigmatic smile
And heavy-lidded eyes instead
Of just a regulation head.

❧ Better In a Bath

Hollie McNish 1983–

in a bath, i'm at my best
in bubbles, even better
this body, all warm-water-wrapped
can weather any weather

if only i could stay there
for conferences and meetings
the school run, first dates
would be so much more relaxing

at awkward adult parties
just lead me to the bathroom
come see me every now and then
as you mingle in the kitchen

even things i love already
would be better in a bath
a train ride; prosecco;
a stroll up to a hilltop path

for now, i'll just lay back
watch the ripples paint the ceiling
float with every deep breath in
add more hot when needed

❧ Celia Celia

Adrian Mitchell 1932–2008

When I am sad and weary
When I think all hope has gone
When I walk along High Holborn
I think of you with nothing on

❧ Bridled Vows

Ian Duhig 1954–

I will be faithful to you, I do vow,
but not until the seas have all run dry
et cetera. Although I mean it now
I'm not a prophet and I will not lie.

To be your perfect wife, I could not swear;
I'll love, yes; honour (maybe); won't obey,
but will co-operate if you will care
as much as you are seeming to today.

I'll do my best to be your better half,
but I don't have the patience of a saint
and at you, not with you, I'll sometimes laugh,
and snap too, though I'll try to show restraint.

We might work out. No blame if we do not.
With all my heart, I think it's worth a shot.

❧ One Perfect Rose

Dorothy Parker 1893–1967

A single flow'r he sent me, since we met.
  All tenderly his messenger he chose;
Deep-hearted, pure, with scented dew still wet—
  One perfect rose.

I knew the language of the floweret;
  "My fragile leaves," it said, "his heart enclose."
Love long has taken for his amulet
  One perfect rose.

Why is it no one ever sent me yet
  One perfect limousine, do you suppose?
Ah no, it's always just my luck to get
  One perfect rose.

ಇ Life Story

Tennessee Williams 1911–1983

After you've been to bed together for the first time,
without the advantage or disadvantage of any prior
    acquaintance,
the other party very often says to you,
Tell me about yourself, I want to know all about you,
what's your story? And you think maybe they really and
    truly do

sincerely want to know your life story, and so you light up
a cigarette and begin to tell it to them, the two of you
lying together in completely relaxed positions
like a pair of rag dolls a bored child dropped on a bed.

You tell them your story, or as much of your story
as time or a fair degree of prudence allows, and they say,
    Oh, oh, oh, oh, oh,
each time a little more faintly, until the oh
is just an audible breath, and then of course

there's some interruption. Slow room service comes up
with a bowl of melting ice cubes, or one of you rises to
    pee
and gaze at himself with the mild astonishment in the
    bathroom mirror.
And then, the first thing you know, before you've had time
to pick up where you left off with your enthralling life
    story,
they're telling you their life story, exactly as they'd
    intended to all along,

and you're saying, Oh, oh, oh, oh, oh,
each time a little more faintly, the vowel at last becoming
no more than an audible sigh,
as the elevator, halfway down the corridor and a turn to
   the left,
draws one last, long, deep breath of exhaustion
and stops breathing forever. Then?

Well, one of you falls asleep
and the other one does likewise with a lighted cigarette in
   his mouth,
and that's how people burn to death in hotel rooms.

❧ How to Triumph Like a Girl

Ada Limón 1976–

I like the lady horses best,
how they make it all look easy,
like running 40 miles per hour
is as fun as taking a nap, or grass.
I like their lady horse swagger,
after winning. Ears up, girls, ears up!
But mainly, let's be honest, I like
that they're ladies. As if this big
dangerous animal is also a part of me,
that somewhere inside the delicate
skin of my body, there pumps
an 8-pound female horse heart,
giant with power, heavy with blood.
Don't you want to believe it?
Don't you want to lift my shirt and see
the huge beating genius machine
that thinks, no, it knows,
it's going to come in first.

❧ Phenomenal Woman

Maya Angelou 1928–2014

Pretty women wonder where my secret lies.
I'm not cute or built to suit a fashion model's size
But when I start to tell them,
They think I'm telling lies.
I say,
It's in the reach of my arms,
The span of my hips,
The stride of my step,
The curl of my lips.
I'm a woman
Phenomenally.
Phenomenal woman,
That's me.

I walk into a room
Just as cool as you please,
And to a man,
The fellows stand or
Fall down on their knees.
Then they swarm around me,
A hive of honey bees.
I say,
It's the fire in my eyes,
And the flash of my teeth,
The swing in my waist,
And the joy in my feet.
I'm a woman
Phenomenally.

Phenomenal woman,
That's me.

Men themselves have wondered
What they see in me.
They try so much
But they can't touch
My inner mystery.
When I try to show them,
They say they still can't see.
I say,
It's in the arch of my back,
The sun of my smile,
The ride of my breasts,
The grace of my style.
I'm a woman
Phenomenally.
Phenomenal woman,
That's me.

Now you understand
Just why my head's not bowed.
I don't shout or jump about
Or have to talk real loud.
When you see me passing,
It ought to make you proud.
I say,
It's in the click of my heels,
The bend of my hair,
the palm of my hand,
The need for my care.
'Cause I'm a woman
Phenomenally.
Phenomenal woman,
That's me.

❧ Into Each Life Some Rain Must Fall

Margaret Fishback 1900–1985

Sometimes I wish that I were dead
 As dead can be, but then again
At times when I've been nicely fed
 On caviar or guinea hen
And I am wearing something new
 And reassuring, I decide
It might be better to eschew
 My tendency to cyanide.

❧ Good Bones

Maggie Smith 1977–

Life is short, though I keep this from my children.
Life is short, and I've shortened mine
in a thousand delicious, ill-advised ways,
a thousand deliciously ill-advised ways
I'll keep from my children. The world is at least
fifty percent terrible, and that's a conservative
estimate, though I keep this from my children.
For every bird there is a stone thrown at a bird.
For every loved child, a child broken, bagged,
sunk in a lake. Life is short and the world
is at least half terrible, and for every kind
stranger, there is one who would break you,
though I keep this from my children. I am trying
to sell them the world. Any decent realtor,
walking you through a real shithole, chirps on
about good bones: This place could be beautiful,
right? You could make this place beautiful.

❧ The Table and the Chair

Edward Lear 1812–1888

I

Said the Table to the Chair,
'You can hardly be aware,
'How I suffer from the heat,
'And from chilblains on my feet!
'If we took a little walk,
'We might have a little talk!
'Pray let us take the air!'
Said the Table to the Chair.

II

Said the Chair unto the Table,
'Now you *know* we are not able!
'How foolishly you talk,
'When you know we *cannot* walk!'
Said the Table, with a sigh,
'It can do no harm to try,
'I've as many legs as you,
'Why can't we walk on two?'

III

So they both went slowly down,
And walked about the town
With a cheerful bumpy sound,
As they toddled round and round.
And everybody cried,
As they hastened to their side,
'See! the Table and the Chair
'Have come out to take the air!'

IV

But in going down an alley,
To a castle in a valley,
They completely lost their way,
And wandered all the day,
Till, to see them safely back,
They paid a Ducky-quack,
And a Beetle, and a Mouse,
Who took them to their house.

V

Then they whispered to each other,
'O delightful little brother!
'What a lovely walk we've taken!
'Let us dine on Beans and Bacon!'
So the Ducky, and the leetle
Browny-Mousy and the Beetle
Dined, and danced upon their heads
Till they toddled to their beds.

🐦 A Brief History of Modern Art in Poetry

Brian Bilston

1. Impressionism

Roses sway in softened reds
Violets swim in murky blues.
Sugar sparkles in the light,
Blurring into golden you.

2. Surrealism

Roses are melting
Violets are too.
Ceci n'est pas le sucre.
Keith is a giant crab.

3. Social Realism

Roses are dead.
Violence is rife.
Don't sugar coat
This bitter life.

4. Abstract Expressionism

5. Pop Art

Roses go BLAM!
Violets go POW!
Sugar is COOL!
You are so WOW!

6. Conceptual Art

Roses are red,
Coated in blood:
A deer's severed head
Drips from above.

❧ Lettuce Marry

Anon

Do you carrot all for me?
My heart beets for you,
With your turnip nose
And your radish face,
You are a peach.
If we cantaloupe,
Lettuce marry:
Weed make a swell pear.

❧ This Is Just To Say

William Carlos Williams 1883–1963

I have eaten
the plums
that were in
the icebox

and which
you were probably
saving
for breakfast

Forgive me
they were delicious
so sweet
and so cold

❧ To the Woman Crying Uncontrollably in the Next Stall

Kim Addonizio 1954–

If you ever woke in your dress at 4am ever
closed your legs to someone you loved opened
them for someone you didn't moved against
a pillow in the dark stood miserably on a beach
seaweed clinging to your ankles paid
good money for a bad haircut backed away
from a mirror that wanted to kill you bled
into the back seat for lack of a tampon
if you swam across a river under rain sang
using a dildo for a microphone stayed up
to watch the moon eat the sun entire
ripped out the stitches in your heart
because why not if you think nothing &
no one can / listen I love you joy is coming

೪ Dreams

Langston Hughes 1901–1967

Hold fast to dreams
For if dreams die
Life is a broken-winged bird
That cannot fly.

Hold fast to dreams
For when dreams go
Life is a barren field
Frozen with snow.

❧ To Hope

John Keats 1795–1821

When by my solitary hearth I sit,
  And hateful thoughts enwrap my soul in gloom;
When no fair dreams before my "mind's eye" flit,
  And the bare heath of life presents no bloom;
Sweet Hope, ethereal balm upon me shed,
And wave thy silver pinions o'er my head!

Whene'er I wander, at the fall of night,
  Where woven boughs shut out the moon's bright ray,
Should sad Despondency my musings fright,
  And frown, to drive fair Cheerfulness away,
Peep with the moonbeams through the leafy roof,
And keep that fiend Despondence far aloof!

Should Disappointment, parent of Despair,
  Strive for her son to seize my careless heart;
When, like a cloud, he sits upon the air,
  Preparing on his spell-bound prey to dart:
Chase him away, sweet Hope, with visage bright,
And fright him as the morning frightens night!

Whene'er the fate of those I hold most dear
  Tells to my fearful breast a tale of sorrow,
O bright-eyed Hope, my morbid fancy cheer;
  Let me awhile thy sweetest comforts borrow:
Thy heaven-born radiance around me shed,
And wave thy silver pinions o'er my head!

Should e'er unhappy love my bosom pain,
  From cruel parents, or relentless fair;
O let me think it is not quite in vain
  To sigh out sonnets to the midnight air!
Sweet Hope, ethereal balm upon me shed,
And wave thy silver pinions o'er my head!

In the long vista of the years to roll,
  Let me not see our country's honour fade:
O let me see our land retain her soul,
  Her pride, her freedom; and not freedom's shade.
From thy bright eyes unusual brightness shed—
Beneath thy pinions canopy my head!

Let me not see the patriot's high bequest,
  Great Liberty! how great in plain attire!
With the base purple of a court oppress'd,
  Bowing her head, and ready to expire:
But let me see thee stoop from heaven on wings
That fill the skies with silver glitterings!

And as, in sparkling majesty, a star
  Gilds the bright summit of some gloomy cloud;
Brightening the half veil'd face of heaven afar:
  So, when dark thoughts my boding spirit shroud,
Sweet Hope, celestial influence round me shed,
Waving thy silver pinions o'er my head!

ঈ Thaw

Edward Thomas 1878–1917

Over the land freckled with snow half-thawed
The speculating rooks at their nests cawed
And saw from elm-tops, delicate as flowers of grass,
What we below could not see, Winter pass.

❧ Four-leaf Clover

Ella Higginson 1861–1940

I know a place where the sun is like gold,
    And the cherry blooms burst with snow,
And down underneath is the loveliest nook,
    Where the four-leaf clovers grow.

One leaf is for hope, and one is for faith,
    And one is for love, you know,
And God put another in for luck—
    If you search, you will find where they grow.

But you must have hope, and you must have faith,
    You must love and be strong – and so—
If you work, if you wait, you will find the place
    Where the four-leaf clovers grow.

❧ "Hope" is the thing with feathers

Emily Dickinson 1830–1886

"Hope" is the thing with feathers –
That perches in the soul –
And sings the tune without the words –
And never stops – at all –

And sweetest – in the Gale – is heard –
And sore must be the storm –
That could abash the little Bird
That kept so many warm –

I've heard it in the chillest land –
And on the strangest Sea –
Yet – never – in Extremity,
It asked a crumb – of me.

❧ Hope

Emily Brontë 1818–1848

Hope was but a timid friend;
   She sat without the grated den,
Watching how my fate would tend,
   Even as selfish-hearted men.

She was cruel in her fear;
   Through the bars, one dreary day,
I looked out to see her there,
   And she turned her face away!

Like a false guard, false watch keeping,
   Still, in strife, she whispered peace;
She would sing while I was weeping;
   If I listened, she would cease.

False she was, and unrelenting;
   When my last joys strewed the ground,
Even Sorrow saw, repenting,
   Those sad relics scattered round;

Hope, whose whisper would have given
   Balm to all my frenzied pain,
Stretched her wings, and soared to heaven,
   Went, and ne'er returned again!

❧ Haiku

Yosa Buson 1716–1783

well now,
if I am to be alone
I'll take the moon as a friend

?❧ Work Without Hope

Samuel Taylor Coleridge 1772–1834

All Nature seems at work. Slugs leave their lair—
The bees are stirring—birds are on the wing—
And Winter slumbering in the open air,
Wears on his smiling face a dream of Spring!
And I the while, the sole unbusy thing,
Nor honey make, nor pair, nor build, nor sing.

Yet well I ken the banks where amaranths blow,
Have traced the fount whence streams of nectar flow.
Bloom, O ye amaranths! bloom for whom ye may,
For me ye bloom not! Glide, rich streams, away!
With lips unbrightened, wreathless brow, I stroll:
And would you learn the spells that drowse my soul?
Work without Hope draws nectar in a sieve,
And Hope without an object cannot live.

❧ The Instinct of Hope

John Clare 1793–1864

Is there another world for this frail dust
To warm with life and be itself again?
Something about me daily speaks there must,
And why should instinct nourish hopes in vain?
'Tis nature's prophesy that such will be,
And everything seems struggling to explain
The close sealed volume of its mystery.
Time wandering onward keeps its usual pace
As seeming anxious of eternity,
To meet that calm and find a resting place.
E'en the small violet feels a future power
And waits each year renewing blooms to bring,
And surely man is no inferior flower
To die unworthy of a second spring?

❧ Say Not the Struggle Nought Availeth

Arthur Hugh Clough 1819–1861

Say not the struggle nought availeth,
   The labour and the wounds are vain,
The enemy faints not, nor faileth,
   And as things have been they remain.

If hopes were dupes, fears may be liars;
   It may be, in yon smoke concealed,
Your comrades chase e'en now the fliers,
   And, but for you, possess the field.

For while the tired waves, vainly breaking
   Seem here no painful inch to gain,
Far back through creeks and inlets making,
   Comes silent, flooding in, the main.

And not by eastern windows only,
   When daylight comes, comes in the light,
In front the sun climbs slow, how slowly,
   But westward, look, the land is bright.

🐦 Spring Has Come Back Again

Rainer Maria Rilke 1875–1926
Translated by Jessie Lamont

Spring has come back again. The earth
is like a child who has memorized
poems, oh, many! . . . now it seems worth
the effort, for she wins the prize.

Her teacher was strict. We loved the white
hair of the old man's beard.
When we ask what the green and the blue are, right
off she knows every word.

Lucky earth, with your holiday,
and all the children coming to play!
We try to catch you. The gayest will do it.

Teacher trained her until she knew it,
and all that's printed in roots and long
unruly stems she sings in song.

❧ A Light Exists in Spring

Emily Dickinson 1830–1886

A light exists in spring
Not present on the Year
At any other period –
When March is scarcely here
A Color stands abroad
On Solitary Fields
That Science cannot overtake,
But Human Nature feels.

It waits upon the Lawn,
It shows the furthest Tree
Upon the furthest Slope you know;
It almost speaks to you.

Then, as Horizons step
Or Noons report away
Without the Formula of sound
It passes, and we stay –

A quality of loss
Affecting our Content,
As Trade had suddenly encroached
Opon a Sacrament –

❧ Instructions on Not Giving Up

Ada Limón 1976–

More than the fuchsia funnels breaking out
of the crabapple tree, more than the neighbor's
almost obscene display of cherry limbs shoving
their cotton candy-colored blossoms to the slate
sky of Spring rains, it's the greening of the trees
that really gets to me. When all the shock of white
and taffy, the world's baubles and trinkets, leave
the pavement strewn with the confetti of aftermath,
the leaves come. Patient, plodding, a green skin
growing over whatever winter did to us, a return
to the strange idea of continuous living despite
the mess of us, the hurt, the empty. Fine then,
I'll take it, the tree seems to say, a new slick leaf
unfurling like a fist to an open palm, I'll take it all.

❧ Tomorrow is Beautiful

Sarah Crossan 1985–

beyond the wall of now,
    tomorrow is waiting.

its light is longing to find you;

    look for its glow
    in the corner you had forgotten.

beyond the cold brick of today
    tomorrow knows better.

it is waffles and blackberries,
    tea and buttered cake,
    it is a robin on your windowsill
    his puffed red belly striving for song.

beyond the hard silence of here,
    tomorrow is beckoning.

it is an unexpected love letter.
it is a long kiss.

it is not crying

    not *always* crying.

because
tomorrow is beautiful.

tomorrow is beautiful.

❧ High Water

Kathleen Jamie 1962–

When the tide returns
From its other life,
bearing its adulterer's gifts

and the wrack-plastered reef
becomes again a sunk unknown,

then we should take our leave –
steering between the telegraph poles
that mark safe channel,

and all the lives we never lived
piled behind us on the shore.

Let them anguish over that! Offspring,
lost friends, our mystified lovers'
sad cries fading in our ears

till the next tide brings us bobbing
back home again – us,
and our shamefaced boat.

April

Nature & Meditation

I T is not entirely clear where the name 'April' came from, although the Ancient Romans came up with competing theories about the month's name (which, to them, was known as Aprilis). Some associated the month with Aphrodite, the Greek name for Venus, the goddess of love; after all, as Charlotte Mew puts it, this loveliest of months brings 'dreams which take [our] breath away'. On the other hand, some believed Aprilis was derived from the Latin '*aperire*', meaning 'to open' – used in the sense that nature's blooms open around this time of year. Modern scholars, however, now believe that neither of these theories were correct, and current thinking is that it came from an ancient root word meaning 'other' – as in, the second month of a year beginning in March, for the earliest Romans did not count January and February in their agricultural year (as mentioned in January, nothing much happens on a farm in the dead of winter). And although today we do not start our calendars in April, with its reminder of Nature's beautiful mutability, it is undeniable that the spring is associated with newness and change. Philip Larkin expresses the wonder of spring's rebirth and renewal in his meditation on 'The Trees' – 'Last year is dead, they seem to say, / Begin afresh, afresh, afresh' – while for William Blake, the birds and lambs appear 'Merrily,/ Merrily, Merrily, to welcome in the year.'

No matter where we are, we can always rely on poetry to transport us to the natural world. Alongside Wordsworth's famous meditation on a field of dancing daffodils, there are countless other works that connect us to countless other memories. Take, for instance, Radclyffe Hall, best known for her novel *The Well of Loneliness* and its ground-breaking portrayal of a lesbian character. Her wistful lyric poem 'On the Hill-Side' recalls watching a lover rest: 'You lay so still in the sunshine, / So still in that hot sweet hour – / That the timid things of the forest land/ Came close; a butterfly lit on your hand,/ Mistaking it for a flower.'

Poetic meditations on nature are often indelibly sweet, reflecting the youthful innocence signified by spring. This is especially the case in Thomas Hardy's charming ballad, 'Wagtail and Baby', where his consistent rhyme scheme imparts a sense of simplicity that belies its formal achievement. Amy Lowell's 'The Pleiades', on the other hand, takes on the voice of a child while marvelling at the constellations –' One group looks like a swarm of bees,/ Papa says they're the Pleiades;/ But I think they must be the toy/ Of some nice little angel boy' – perhaps precisely because this is the most effective way to emulate how struck we are with their wonder. Stellar taxonomies cannot quell the deeply imaginative mood that nature's spectacles evoke. For Gerard Manley Hopkins, however, the relation between spring and innocence is more explicit; the spring is 'A strain of the earth's sweet being in the beginning / In Eden garden', a glimpse of prelapsarian life. And in a similar vein, for Lord Byron, the pleasure one feels is not simply inno-cent but also innate; the 'pleasure' derived from 'pathless woods' and unspoilt nature is the pleasure of feeling oneself 'mingle with the Universe', of being connected to all living things.

Of course, this is not always the case – the poems in this month represent nature in all of its glory, and nature is not always sweet. Towards the end of the month come two poems about the mosquito, that most familiar of summertime pests, by two disparate poets; the modernist D.H. Lawrence and the Japanese haiku master, Kobayashi Issa. So too are there some poets who are gloomy about the spring;

William Cowper's 'The Shrubbery' is almost comically miserable, claiming nature's 'fruitful scenes' 'tell [him] of enjoyments past, / And those of sorrows yet to come', while Edna St. Vincent Millay grimly observes that 'April/ Comes like an idiot, babbling and strewing flowers'.

But whatever a poet takes as their subject, for the reader concentrating on a poem is a meditative gift that slows down time or even crystallises a moment, as with Issa's haiku. The environmentalist Wendell Berry's poem, 'The Peace of Wild Things', highlights how both poetry and nature can offer reprieve in our despair, by encouraging us to live in the moment: 'I come to into the peace of wild things/ who do not tax their lives with forethought/ of grief. [. . .] For a time/ I rest in the grace of the world, and am free.' Later in the month, Charlotte Mew echoes this idea: 'I'll like the Spring because it is simply Spring/ As the thrushes do.' It is advice, perhaps, that Cowper should have taken.

For oft, when on my couch I lie
In vacant or in pensive mood,
They flash upon that inward eye
Which is the bliss of solitude;
And then my heart with pleasure fills,
And dances with the daffodils.

William Wordsworth

ॐ The Peace of Wild Things

Wendell Berry 1934–

When despair for the world grows in me
and I wake in the night at the least sound
in fear of what my life and my children's lives may be,
I go and lie down where the wood drake
rests in his beauty on the water, and the great heron feeds.
I come into the peace of wild things
who do not tax their lives with forethought
of grief. I come into the presence of still water.
And I feel above me the day-blind stars
waiting with their light. For a time
I rest in the grace of the world, and am free.

❧ There is a Pleasure in the Pathless Woods

Lord Byron 1788–1824

There is a pleasure in the pathless woods,
There is a rapture on the lonely shore,
There is society where none intrudes,
By the deep Sea, and music in its roar:
I love not Man the less, but Nature more,
From these our interviews, in which I steal
From all I may be, or have been before,
To mingle with the Universe, and feel
What I can ne'er express, yet cannot all conceal.

Roll on, thou deep and dark blue Ocean—roll!
Ten thousand fleets sweep over thee in vain;
Man marks the earth with ruin—his control
Stops with the shore;—upon the watery plain
The wrecks are all thy deed, nor doth remain
A shadow of man's ravage, save his own,
When for a moment, like a drop of rain,
He sinks into thy depths with bubbling groan,
Without a grave, unknelled, uncoffined, and unknown.

His steps are not upon thy paths,—thy fields
Are not a spoil for him,—thou dost arise
And shake him from thee; the vile strength he wields
For earth's destruction thou dost all despise,
Spurning him from thy bosom to the skies,
And send'st him, shivering in thy playful spray
And howling, to his gods, where haply lies
His petty hope in some near port or bay,
And dashest him again to earth:—there let him lay.

❧ I Wandered Lonely as a Cloud

William Wordsworth 1770–1850

I wandered lonely as a cloud
That floats on high o'er vales and hills,
When all at once I saw a crowd,
A host, of golden daffodils;
Beside the lake, beneath the trees,
Fluttering and dancing in the breeze.

Continuous as the stars that shine
And twinkle on the milky way,
They stretched in never-ending line
Along the margin of a bay:
Ten thousand saw I at a glance,
Tossing their heads in sprightly dance.

The waves beside them danced; but they
Out-did the sparkling waves in glee:
A poet could not but be gay,
In such a jocund company:
I gazed—and gazed—but little thought
What wealth the show to me had brought:

For oft, when on my couch I lie
In vacant or in pensive mood,
They flash upon that inward eye
Which is the bliss of solitude;
And then my heart with pleasure fills,
And dances with the daffodils.

❧ Home-Thoughts, from Abroad

Robert Browning 1812–1889

Oh, to be in England
Now that April's there,
And whoever wakes in England
Sees, some morning, unaware,
That the lowest boughs and the brushwood sheaf
Round the elm-tree bole are in tiny leaf,
While the chaffinch sings on the orchard bough
In England—now!

And after April, when May follows,
And the whitethroat builds, and all the swallows!
Hark, where my blossomed pear-tree in the hedge
Leans to the field and scatters on the clover
Blossoms and dewdrops—at the bent spray's edge—
That's the wise thrush; he sings each song twice over,
Lest you should think he never could recapture
The first fine careless rapture!
And though the fields look rough with hoary dew,
All will be gay when noontide wakes anew
The buttercups, the little children's dower
—Far brighter than this gaudy melon-flower!

❧ The Pleiades

Amy Lowell 1874–1925

By day you cannot see the sky
For it is up so very high.
You look and look, but it's so blue
That you can never see right through.

But when night comes it is quite plain,
And all the stars are there again.
They seem just like old friends to me,
I've known them all my life you see.

There is the dipper first, and there
Is Cassiopeia in her chair,
Orion's belt, the Milky Way,
And lots I know but cannot say.

One group looks like a swarm of bees,
Papa says they're the Pleiades;
But I think they must be the toy
Of some nice little angel boy.

Perhaps his jackstones which to-day
He has forgot to put away,
And left them lying on the sky
Where he will find them bye and bye

I wish he'd come and play with me.
We'd have such fun, for it would be
A most unusual thing for boys
To feel that they had stars for toys!

❧ Lines Composed a Few Miles above Tintern Abbey, On Revisiting the Banks of the Wye during a Tour. July 13, 1798

William Wordsworth 1770–1850

Five years have past; five summers, with the length
Of five long winters! and again I hear
These waters, rolling from their mountain-springs
With a soft inland murmur.—Once again
Do I behold these steep and lofty cliffs,
That on a wild secluded scene impress
Thoughts of more deep seclusion; and connect
The landscape with the quiet of the sky.
The day is come when I again repose
Here, under this dark sycamore, and view
These plots of cottage-ground, these orchard-tufts,
Which at this season, with their unripe fruits,
Are clad in one green hue, and lose themselves
'Mid groves and copses. Once again I see
These hedge-rows, hardly hedge-rows, little lines
Of sportive wood run wild: these pastoral farms,
Green to the very door; and wreaths of smoke
Sent up, in silence, from among the trees!
With some uncertain notice, as might seem
Of vagrant dwellers in the houseless woods,
Or of some Hermit's cave, where by his fire
The Hermit sits alone.

These beauteous forms,
Through a long absence, have not been to me
As is a landscape to a blind man's eye:
But oft, in lonely rooms, and 'mid the din
Of towns and cities, I have owed to them,
In hours of weariness, sensations sweet,
Felt in the blood, and felt along the heart;
And passing even into my purer mind
With tranquil restoration:—feelings too
Of unremembered pleasure: such, perhaps,
As have no slight or trivial influence
On that best portion of a good man's life,
His little, nameless, unremembered, acts
Of kindness and of love. Nor less, I trust,
To them I may have owed another gift,
Of aspect more sublime; that blessed mood,
In which the burthen of the mystery,
In which the heavy and the weary weight
Of all this unintelligible world,
Is lightened:—that serene and blessed mood,
In which the affections gently lead us on,—
Until, the breath of this corporeal frame
And even the motion of our human blood
Almost suspended, we are laid asleep
In body, and become a living soul:
While with an eye made quiet by the power
Of harmony, and the deep power of joy,
We see into the life of things.

                                         If this
Be but a vain belief, yet, oh! how oft—
In darkness and amid the many shapes
Of joyless daylight; when the fretful stir
Unprofitable, and the fever of the world,
Have hung upon the beatings of my heart—
How oft, in spirit, have I turned to thee,
O sylvan Wye! thou wanderer thro' the woods,
   How often has my spirit turned to thee!

   And now, with gleams of half-extinguished thought,
With many recognitions dim and faint,
And somewhat of a sad perplexity,
The picture of the mind revives again:
While here I stand, not only with the sense
Of present pleasure, but with pleasing thoughts
That in this moment there is life and food
For future years. And so I dare to hope,
Though changed, no doubt, from what I was when first
I came among these hills; when like a roe
I bounded o'er the mountains, by the sides
Of the deep rivers, and the lonely streams,
Wherever nature led: more like a man
Flying from something that he dreads, than one
Who sought the thing he loved. For nature then
(The coarser pleasures of my boyish days
And their glad animal movements all gone by)
To me was all in all.—I cannot paint
What then I was. The sounding cataract
Haunted me like a passion: the tall rock,
The mountain, and the deep and gloomy wood,
Their colours and their forms, were then to me
An appetite; a feeling and a love,
That had no need of a remoter charm,

By thought supplied, nor any interest
Unborrowed from the eye.——That time is past,
And all its aching joys are now no more,
And all its dizzy raptures. Not for this
Faint I, nor mourn nor murmur; other gifts
Have followed; for such loss, I would believe,
Abundant recompense. For I have learned
To look on nature, not as in the hour
Of thoughtless youth; but hearing oftentimes
The still sad music of humanity,
Nor harsh nor grating, though of ample power
To chasten and subdue.——And I have felt
A presence that disturbs me with the joy
Of elevated thoughts; a sense sublime
Of something far more deeply interfused,
Whose dwelling is the light of setting suns,
And the round ocean and the living air,
And the blue sky, and in the mind of man:
A motion and a spirit, that impels
All thinking things, all objects of all thought,
And rolls through all things. Therefore am I still
A lover of the meadows and the woods
And mountains; and of all that we behold
From this green earth; of all the mighty world
Of eye, and ear,——both what they half create,
And what perceive; well pleased to recognise
In nature and the language of the sense
The anchor of my purest thoughts, the nurse,
The guide, the guardian of my heart, and soul
Of all my moral being.

                    Nor perchance,
If I were not thus taught, should I the more
Suffer my genial spirits to decay:
For thou art with me here upon the banks
Of this fair river; thou my dearest Friend,
My dear, dear Friend; and in thy voice I catch
The language of my former heart, and read
My former pleasures in the shooting lights
Of thy wild eyes. Oh! yet a little while
May I behold in thee what I was once,
My dear, dear Sister! and this prayer I make,
Knowing that Nature never did betray
The heart that loved her; 'tis her privilege,
Through all the years of this our life, to lead
From joy to joy: for she can so inform
The mind that is within us, so impress
With quietness and beauty, and so feed
With lofty thoughts, that neither evil tongues,
Rash judgments, nor the sneers of selfish men,
Nor greetings where no kindness is, nor all
The dreary intercourse of daily life,
Shall e'er prevail against us, or disturb
Our cheerful faith, that all which we behold
Is full of blessings. Therefore let the moon
Shine on thee in thy solitary walk;
And let the misty mountain-winds be free
To blow against thee: and, in after years,
When these wild ecstasies shall be matured
Into a sober pleasure; when thy mind
Shall be a mansion for all lovely forms,
Thy memory be as a dwelling-place
For all sweet sounds and harmonies; oh! then,
If solitude, or fear, or pain, or grief,
Should be thy portion, with what healing thoughts

Of tender joy wilt thou remember me,
And these my exhortations! Nor, perchance—
If I should be where I no more can hear
Thy voice, nor catch from thy wild eyes these gleams
Of past existence—wilt thou then forget
That on the banks of this delightful stream
We stood together; and that I, so long
A worshipper of Nature, hither came
Unwearied in that service: rather say
With warmer love—oh! with far deeper zeal
Of holier love. Nor wilt thou then forget,
That after many wanderings, many years
Of absence, these steep woods and lofty cliffs,
And this green pastoral landscape, were to me
More dear, both for themselves and for thy sake!

❧ On a Lane in Spring

John Clare 1793–1864

A Little Lane, the brook runs close beside
And spangles in the sunshine while the fish glide swiftly by
And hedges leafing with the green spring tide
From out their greenery the old birds fly
And chirp and whistle in the morning sun
The pilewort glitters 'neath the pale blue sky
The little robin has its nest begun
And grass green linnets round the bushes fly
– How Mild the Spring Comes in – the daisy buds
Lift up their golden blossoms to the sky
How lovely are the pingles and the woods
Here a beetle runs – and there a fly
Rests on the Arum leaf in bottle green
And all the Spring in this Sweet lane is seen

❧ Spring

Gerard Manley Hopkins 1844–1889

Nothing is so beautiful as Spring –
   When weeds, in wheels, shoot long and lovely and lush;
   Thrush's eggs look little low heavens, and thrush
Through the echoing timber does so rinse and wring
The ear, it strikes like lightnings to hear him sing;
   The glassy peartree leaves and blooms, they brush
   The descending blue; that blue is all in a rush
With richness; the racing lambs too have fair their fling.

What is all this juice and all this joy?
   A strain of the earth's sweet being in the beginning
In Eden garden. – Have, get, before it cloy,
   Before it cloud, Christ, lord, and sour with sinning,
Innocent mind and Mayday in girl and boy,
   Most, O maid's child, thy choice and worthy the winning.

❧ Spring

William Blake 1757–1827

Sound the Flute!
Now it's mute.
Birds delight
Day and Night;
Nightingale
In the dale,
Lark in Sky,
Merrily,
Merrily, Merrily, to welcome in the Year.

Little Boy,
Full of joy;
Little Girl,
Sweet and small;
Cock does crow,
So do you;
Merry voice,
Infant noise,
Merrily, Merrily, to welcome in the Year.

Little Lamb,
Here I am;
Come and lick
My white neck;
Let me pull
Your soft Wool;
Ket me kiss
Your soft face:
Merrily, Merrily, we welcome in the Year.

❧ I come weary

Matsuo Bashō 1644–1694
Translated by William George Aston

I come weary,
In search of an inn—
Ah! These wisteria flowers!

❧ Spring Song

Edith Nesbit 1858–1924

All winter through I sat alone,
Doors barred and windows shuttered fast,
And listened to the wind's faint moan,
And ghostly mutterings of the past;
And in the pauses of the rain,
'Mid whispers of dead sorrow and sin,
Love tapped upon the window pane:
I had no heart to let him in.

But now, with spring, my doors stand wide;
My windows let delight creep through;
I hear the skylark sing outside;
I see the crocus, golden new.
The pigeons on my window-sill,
Winging and wooing, flirt and flout,—
Now Love must enter if he will,
I have no heart to keep him out.

❧ The Downs

John Galsworthy 1867–1933

O the Down high to the cool sky;
And the feel of the sun-warmed moss!
And each cardoon, like a full moon
Fairy-spun of the thistle floss;
And the beech-grove, and a wood-dove,
And the trail where the shepherds pass;
And the lark's song, and the wind-song,
And the scent of the parching grass!

🐦 The Trees

Philip Larkin 1922–1985

The trees are coming into leaf
Like something almost being said;
The recent buds relax and spread,
Their greenness is a kind of grief.

Is it that they are born again
And we grow old? No, they die too,
Their yearly trick of looking new
Is written down in rings of grain.

Yet still the unresting castles thresh
In fullgrown thickness every May.
Last year is dead, they seem to say,
Begin afresh, afresh, afresh.

❧ Spring

Edna St. Vincent Millay 1892–1950

To what purpose, April, do you return again?
Beauty is not enough.
You can no longer quiet me with the redness
Of little leaves opening stickily.
I know what I know.
The sun is hot on my neck as I observe
The spikes of the crocus.
The smell of the earth is good.
It is apparent that there is no death.
But what does that signify?
Not only under ground are the brains of men
Eaten by maggots.
Life in itself
Is nothing,
An empty cup, a flight of uncarpeted stairs.
It is not enough that yearly, down this hill,
April
Comes like an idiot, babbling and strewing flowers.

❧ The Brook

Alfred, Lord Tennyson 1809–1892

I come from haunts of coot and hern,
I make a sudden sally,
And sparkle out among the fern,
To bicker down a valley.

By thirty hills I hurry down,
Or slip between the ridges,
By twenty thorps, a little town,
And half a hundred bridges.

Till last by Philip's farm I flow
To join the brimming river,
For men may come and men may go,
But I go on for ever.

I chatter over stony ways,
In little sharps and trebles,
I bubble into eddying bays,
I babble on the pebbles.

With many a curve my banks I fret
By many a field and fallow,
And many a fairy foreland set
With willow-weed and mallow.

I chatter, chatter, as I flow
To join the brimming river,
For men may come and men may go,
But I go on for ever.

I wind about, and in and out,
　　With here a blossom sailing,
And here and there a lusty trout,
　　And here and there a grayling,

And here and there a foamy flake
　　Upon me, as I travel
With many a silver waterbreak
　　Above the golden gravel,

And draw them all along, and flow
　　To join the brimming river,
For men may come and men may go,
　　But I go on forever.

I steal by lawns and grassy plots,
　　I slide by hazel covers;
I move the sweet forget-me-nots
　　That grow for happy lovers.

I slip, I slide, I gloom, I glance,
　　Among my skimming swallows;
I make the netted sunbeam dance
　　Against my sandy shallows.

I murmur under moon and stars
　　In brambly wildernesses;
I linger by my shingly bars;
　　I loiter round my cresses;

And out again I curve and flow
　　To join the brimming river,
For men may come and men may go,
　　But I go on for ever.

❧ I so liked Spring

Charlotte Mew 1869–1928

I so liked Spring last year
Because you were here; –
The thrushes too –
Because it was these you so liked to hear –
I so liked you.

This year's a different thing, –
I'll not think of you.
But I'll like the Spring because it is simply Spring
As the thrushes do.

❧ Tall Nettles

Edward Thomas 1878–1917

Tall nettles cover up, as they have done
These many springs, the rusty harrow, the plough
Long worn out, and the roller made of stone:
Only the elm butt tops the nettles now.
This corner of the farmyard I like most:
As well as any bloom upon a flower
I like the dust on the nettles, never lost
Except to prove the sweetness of a shower.

❧ Meeting at Night

Robert Browning 1812–1889

I

The grey sea and the long black land;
And the yellow half-moon large and low;
And the startled little waves that leap
In fiery ringlets from their sleep,
As I gain the cove with pushing prow,
And quench its speed i' the slushy sand.

II

Then a mile of warm sea-scented beach;
Three fields to cross till a farm appears;
A tap at the pane, the quick sharp scratch
And blue spurt of a lighted match,
And a voice less loud, thro' its joys and fears,
Than the two hearts beating each to each!

❧ In the Fields

Charlotte Mew 1869–1928

Lord, when I look at lovely things which pass,
Under old trees the shadows of young leaves
Dancing to please the wind along the grass,
Or the gold stillness of the August sun on the August
    sheaves;
Can I believe there is a heavenlier world than this?
And if there is
Will the strange heart of any everlasting thing
Bring me these dreams which take my breath away?
They come at evening with the home-flying rooks and the
    scent of hay,
Over the fields. They come in Spring.

❧ The Shrubbery

William Cowper 1731–1800

Oh happy shades—to me unblest!
Friendly to peace, but not to me!
How ill the scene that offers rest,
And heart that cannot rest, agree!

This glassy stream, that spreading pine,
Those alders quiv'ring to the breeze,
Might sooth a soul less hurt than mine,
And please, if any thing could please.

But fix'd unalterable care
Foregoes not what she feels within,
Shows the same sadness ev'rywhere,
And slights the season and the scene.

For all that pleas'd in wood or lawn,
While peace possess'd these silent bow'rs,
Her animating smile withdrawn,
Has lost its beauties and its pow'rs.

The saint or moralist should tread
This moss-grown alley, musing, slow;
They seek, like me, the secret shade,
But not, like me, to nourish woe!

Me fruitful scenes and prospects waste
Alike admonish not to roam;
These tell me of enjoyments past,
And those of sorrows yet to come.

❧ Nature and Man *from* Queen Mab

Percy Bysshe Shelley 1792–1822

Look on yonder earth:
The golden harvests spring; the unfailing sun
Sheds light and life; the fruits, the flowers, the trees,
Arise in due succession; all things speak
Peace, harmony, and love. The universe,
In nature's silent eloquence, declares
That all fulfil the works of love and joy, –
All but the outcast man.

🎋 Trees in the Garden

D.H. Lawrence 1885–1930

Ah in the thunder air
how still the trees are!

And the lime-tree, lovely and tall, every leaf silent
hardly looses even a last breath of perfume.

And the ghostly, creamy coloured little tree of leaves
white, ivory white among the rambling greens
how evanescent, variegated elder, she hesitates on the
    green grass
as if, in another moment, she would disappear
with all her grace of foam!

And the larch that is only a column, it goes up too tall to
    see:
and the balsam-pines that are blue with the grey-blue
    blueness of things from the sea,
and the young copper beech, its leaves red-rosy at the ends
how still they are together, they stand so still
in the thunder air, all strangers to one another
as the green grass glows upwards, strangers in the silent
    garden.

❧ Wenlock Edge (A Shropshire Lad 31)

A.E. Housman 1859–1936

On Wenlock Edge the wood's in trouble;
   His forest fleece the Wrekin heaves;
The gale, it plies the saplings double,
   And thick on Severn snow the leaves.

'Twould blow like this through holt and hanger
   When Uricon the city stood:
'Tis the old wind in the old anger,
   But then it threshed another wood.

Then, 'twas before my time, the Roman
   At yonder heaving hill would stare:
The blood that warms an English yeoman,
   The thoughts that hurt him, they were there.

There, like the wind through woods in riot,
   Through him the gale of life blew high;
The tree of man was never quiet:
   Then 'twas the Roman, now 'tis I.

The gale, it plies the saplings double,
   It blows so hard, 'twill soon be gone:
To-day the Roman and his trouble
   Are ashes under Uricon.

೪ On the Hill-Side

Radclyffe Hall 1880–1943

A Memory

You lay so still in the sunshine,
So still in that hot sweet hour—
That the timid things of the forest land
Came close; a butterfly lit on your hand,
Mistaking it for a flower.

You scarcely breathed in your slumber,
So dreamless it was, so deep—
While the warm air stirred in my veins like wine,
The air that had blown through a jasmine vine,
But you slept—and I let you sleep.

❧ Wagtail and Baby

Thomas Hardy 1840–1928

A baby watched a ford, whereto
A wagtail came for drinking;
A blaring bull went wading through,
The wagtail showed no shrinking.

A stallion splashed his way across,
The birdie nearly sinking;
He gave his plumes a twitch and toss,
And held his own unblinking.

Next saw the baby round the spot
A mongrel slowly slinking;
The wagtail gazed, but faltered not
In dip and sip and prinking.

A perfect gentleman then neared;
The wagtail, in a winking,
With terror rose and disappeared;
The baby fell a-thinking.

❧ The Woodspurge

Dante Gabriel Rossetti 1828–1882

The wind flapp'd loose, the wind was still,
Shaken out dead from tree and hill:
I had walk'd on at the wind's will,—
I sat now, for the wind was still.

Between my knees my forehead was,—
My lips, drawn in, said not Alas!
My hair was over in the grass,
My naked ears heard the day pass.

My eyes, wide open, had the run
Of some ten weeds to fix upon;
Among those few, out of the sun,
The woodspurge flower'd, three cups in one.

From perfect grief there need not be
Wisdom or even memory:
One thing then learnt remains to me,—
The woodspurge has a cup of three.

❧ The Tyger

William Blake 1757–1827

Tyger Tyger, burning bright,
In the forests of the night;
What immortal hand or eye,
Could frame thy fearful symmetry?

In what distant deeps or skies.
Burnt the fire of thine eyes?
On what wings dare he aspire?
What the hand, dare seize the fire?

And what shoulder, & what art,
Could twist the sinews of thy heart?
And when thy heart began to beat.
What dread hand? & what dread feet?

What the hammer? what the chain,
In what furnace was thy brain?
What the anvil? what dread grasp.
Dare its deadly terrors clasp?

When the stars threw down their spears
And water'd heaven with their tears:
Did he smile his work to see?
Did he who made the Lamb make thee?

Tyger Tyger burning bright,
In the forests of the night:
What immortal hand or eye,
Dare frame thy fearful symmetry?

❧ The Eagle

Alfred, Lord Tennyson 1809–1892

He clasps the crag with crooked hands;
Close to the sun in lonely lands,
Ring'd with the azure world, he stands.

The wrinkled sea beneath him crawls;
He watches from his mountain walls,
And like a thunderbolt he falls.

❧ The Mosquito

D.H. Lawrence 1885–1930

When did you start your tricks
Monsieur?

What do you stand on such high legs for?
Why this length of shredded shank
You exaltation?

Is it so that you shall lift your centre of gravity upwards
And weigh no more than air as you alight upon me,
Stand upon me weightless, you phantom?

I heard a woman call you the Winged Victory
In sluggish Venice.
You turn your head towards your tail, and smile.

How can you put so much devilry
Into that translucent phantom shred
Of a frail corpus?

Queer, with your thin wings and your streaming legs
How you sail like a heron, or a dull clot of air,
A nothingness.

Yet what an aura surrounds you;
Your evil little aura, prowling, and casting a numbness on
    my mind.

That is your trick, your bit of filthy magic:
Invisibility, and the anæsthetic power
To deaden my attention in your direction.

But I know your game now, streaky sorcerer.

Queer, how you stalk and prowl the air
In circles and evasions, enveloping me,
Ghoul on wings
Winged Victory.

Settle, and stand on long thin shanks
Eyeing me sideways, and cunningly conscious that I am
    aware,
You speck.

I hate the way you lurch off sideways into air
Having read my thoughts against you.

Come then, let us play at unawares,
And see who wins in this sly game of bluff.
Man or mosquito.

You don't know that I exist, and I don't know that you
    exist.
Now then!

It is your trump
It is your hateful little trump
You pointed fiend,
Which shakes my sudden blood to hatred of you:
It is your small, high, hateful bugle in my ear.

Why do you do it?
Surely it is bad policy.

They say you can't help it.

If that is so, then I believe a little in Providence protecting
    the innocent.
But it sounds so amazingly like a slogan
A yell of triumph as you snatch my scalp.

Blood, red blood
Super-magical
Forbidden liquor.

I behold you stand
For a second enspasmed in oblivion,
Obscenely ecstasied
Sucking live blood
My blood.

Such silence, such suspended transport,
Such gorging,
Such obscenity of trespass.

You stagger
As well as you may.
Only your accursed hairy frailty
Your own imponderable weightlessness
Saves you, wafts you away on the very draught my anger
    makes in its snatching.

Away with a pæan of derision
You winged blood-drop.
Can I not overtake you?
Are you one too many for me
Winged Victory?
Am I not mosquito enough to out-mosquito you?

Queer, what a big stain my sucked blood makes
Beside the infinitesimal faint smear of you!
Queer, what a dim dark smudge you have disappeared
    into!

❧ Mosquito at my ear

Kobayashi Issa 1763–1828
Translated by Robert Hass

Mosquito at my ear—
does he think
I'm deaf?

May

Gratitude

N AMED after Maia, the Roman goddess of growth, May is a
month that people have long celebrated for its beauty and
used as a time to give thanks. In ancient Greece, one of the
chief Athenian festivals, Thargelia, was celebrated around the end of
May. People would offer the first fruits of the earth to Helios, their sun
god. This was partly to appease him and prevent excessive heat, which
could destroy their crops, but it was also a thanksgiving celebration
and a time to express gratitude for the sun's return after the winter.

Throughout Europe's history, there have also been other celebrations, from the Gaelic festival of Beltaine to May Day, and to the
ninth-century Carolingian Emperor Charlemagne, May was known as
'wunnimanoth', meaning 'joy-month'. The seemingly ceaseless store
of poems celebrating the month are represented here with works by
some of the most enduring English poets, starting with Thomas
Dekker's ecstatic ode on 'The month of May, the merry month of May,/
So frolic, so gay, and so green, so green, so green!' Dekker's poem is
followed with pieces by John Milton, Lord Tennyson and William
Wordsworth. All of them associate the month with rural courtship in
some way, whether Milton's 'warm desire', Tennyson's hoards of 'shepherd lad' suitors, or Wordsworth's lovebird 'paramours'. William
Shakespeare, for his part, turns this tradition on its head with his most

celebrated sonnet; the seasons, he says, fade 'by chance or nature's changing course,' but his love's 'eternal summer shall not fade.' But the writing collected for this month is by no means drawn from homogenous sources. Also included in this month are thanksgiving prayers from various cultures; whether prayers drawn from the Lakota people, the Haudenosaunee people, or the modern Siddha Yoga movement, all emphasise being grateful for the universe that surrounds us.

Poetry is a powerful medium that connects us to the greatest of human wisdom. A recurrent theme throughout the ages has always been an emphasis on the importance of finding gratitude within ourselves, even in uneasy times. The thirteenth-century Persian poet Rumi reminds us in 'The Guest House' that there are opportunities even in our hardships. Each moment and each experience is a guest in our lives, and we should welcome them all with open arms: 'Be grateful for whoever comes, / because each has been sent / as a guide from beyond.' The fact that Rumi remains a best-selling poet even today is testament to the enduring strength of his message. From more recent times, a similar message has been echoed by the Palestinian-American poet Naomi Shihab Nye, in the poem 'Kindness', where she suggests our sorrows provide the necessary foundation to appreciate that which is good: 'Before you know what kindness really is / you must lose things, / feel the future dissolve in a moment / like salt in a weakened broth.'

Also common is the theme of appreciating that which we do not enjoy. It appears in the work of another poet, like Rumi, with extraordinarily wide appeal: the early-twentieth century Lebanese poet, Khalil Gibran. Taken from *The Prophet*, a book of his prose poetry that has been translated into over one hundred languages since its original publication in 1923, Gibran's piece 'On Work' offers a refreshing perspective on the most mundane of subjects: 'When you work you are a flute through whose heart the whispering of the hours turns to music. / Which of you would be a reed, dumb and silent, when all else sings together in unison? / Always you have been told that work is a curse and labour a misfortune. / But I say to you that when you work you fulfil a part of earth's furthest dream.' Max Ehrmann conveys a similar message with the reminder in 'Desiderata' to 'Enjoy your achievements as well as your plans./ Keep interested in your own career, however humble;/ it is a real possession in the changing fortunes of time.'

Even if there is nothing to be grateful for, we can try to forget the things which weigh us down; envy, vengeance, want. This is the message conveyed by the Polish-American poet, Czesław Miłosz. When awarding him the Nobel Prize in Literature in 1980, the Swedish Academy aptly described how his poetry 'voices man's exposed condition in a world of severe conflicts'. Yet in 'Gift,' gratitude is ultimately introspective, taking the simple form of not wanting: 'There was no thing on earth I wanted to possess./ I knew no one worth my envying him./ Whatever evil I had suffered, I forgot.'

When the world feels like a battleground, expressing gratitude can help us to feel more grounded and fulfilled. The gift of poetry is that reading it forces us to stop and recall that no matter how trifling or small, there is always something to be grateful for – be it the sight of wild geese heading home, hummingbirds stopping over honeysuckle flowers or an orange shared at lunch.

I look
at you and I would rather look at you
than all the portraits in the world

Frank O'Hara

❧ Wild Geese

Mary Oliver 1935–2019

You do not have to be good.
You do not have to walk on your knees
for a hundred miles through the desert repenting.
You only have to let the soft animal of your body
  love what it loves.
Tell me about despair, yours, and I will tell you mine.
Meanwhile the world goes on.
Meanwhile the sun and the clear pebbles of the rain
are moving across the landscapes,
over the prairies and the deep trees,
the mountains and the rivers.
Meanwhile the wild geese, high in the clean blue air,
are heading home again.
Whoever you are, no matter how lonely,
the world offers itself to your imagination,
calls to you like the wild geese, harsh and exciting –
over and over announcing your place
in the family of things.

🐦 My Brilliant Image

Hafez 1325–1390

One day the sun admitted
I am just a shadow.
I wish I could show you
The infinite incandescence
That has cast my brilliant image!
I wish I could show you,
When you are lonely or in darkness,
The Astonishing Light
Of your own Being!

❧ i thank You God for most this amazing

E.E. Cummings 1894–1962

i thank You God for most this amazing
day: for the leaping greenly spirits of trees
and a blue true dream of sky; and for everything
which is natural which is infinite which is yes

(i who have died am alive again today,
and this is the sun's birthday; this is the birth
day of life and of love and wings: and of the gay
great happening illimitably earth)

how should tasting touching hearing seeing
breathing any—lifted from the no
of all nothing—human merely being
doubt unimaginable You?

(now the ears of my ears awake and
now the eyes of my eyes are opened)

🐦 Gift

Czesław Miłosz 1911–2004

A day so happy.
Fog lifted early, I worked in the garden.
Hummingbirds were stopping over honeysuckle flowers.
There was no thing on earth I wanted to possess.
I knew no one worth my envying him.
Whatever evil I had suffered, I forgot.
To think that once I was the same man did not embarrass
  me.
In my body I felt no pain.
When straightening up, I saw the blue sea and sails.

❧ The Wonderful World

William Brighty Rands 1823–1882

Great, wide, beautiful, wonderful World,
With the wonderful water round you curled,
And the wonderful grass upon your breast—
World, you are beautifully dressed!

The wonderful air is over me,
And the wonderful wind is shaking the tree,–
It walks on the water, and whirls the mills,
And talks to itself on the tops of the hills.

You friendly Earth, how far do you go,
With the wheat-fields that nod and the rivers that flow,
With cities and gardens, and cliffs, and isles,
And people upon you for thousands of miles?

Ah! you are so great, and I am so small,
I hardly can think of you, World, at all;
And yet, when I said my prayers to-day,
My mother kissed me, and said, quite gay,

"If the wonderful World is great to you,
And great to father and mother, too,
You are more than the Earth, though you are such a dot!
You can love and think, and the Earth cannot!"

ஂ Kindness

Naomi Shihab Nye 1952–

Before you know what kindness really is
you must lose things,
feel the future dissolve in a moment
like salt in a weakened broth.
What you held in your hand,
what you counted and carefully saved,
all this must go so you know
how desolate the landscape can be
between the regions of kindness.
How you ride and ride
thinking the bus will never stop,
the passengers eating maize and chicken
will stare out the window forever.

Before you learn the tender gravity of kindness
you must travel where the Indian in a white poncho
lies dead by the side of the road.
You must see how this could be you,
how he too was someone
who journeyed through the night with plans
and the simple breath that kept him alive.

Before you know kindness as the deepest thing inside,
you must know sorrow as the other deepest thing.
You must wake up with sorrow.
You must speak to it till your voice
catches the thread of all sorrows
and you see the size of the cloth.
Then it is only kindness that makes sense anymore,
only kindness that ties your shoes
and sends you out into the day to gaze at bread,
only kindness that raises its head
from the crowd of the world to say
It is I you have been looking for,
and then goes with you everywhere
like a shadow or a friend.

❧ Japanese Maple

Clive James 1939–2019

Your death, near now, is of an easy sort.
So slow a fading out brings no real pain.
Breath growing short
Is just uncomfortable. You feel the drain
Of energy, but thought and sight remain:

Enhanced, in fact. When did you ever see
So much sweet beauty as when fine rain falls
On that small tree
And saturates your brick back garden walls,
So many Amber Rooms and mirror halls?

Ever more lavish as the dusk descends
This glistening illuminates the air.
It never ends.
Whenever the rain comes it will be there,
Beyond my time, but now I take my share.

My daughter's choice, the maple tree is new.
Come autumn and its leaves will turn to flame.
What I must do
Is live to see that. That will end the game
For me, though life continues all the same:

Filling the double doors to bathe my eyes,
A final flood of colours will live on
As my mind dies,
Burned by my vision of a world that shone
So brightly at the last, and then was gone.

❧ Loveliest of trees, the cherry now (A Shropshire Lad 2)

A.E. Housman 1859–1936

Loveliest of trees, the cherry now
Is hung with bloom along the bough,
And stands about the woodland ride
Wearing white for Eastertide.

Now, of my threescore years and ten,
Twenty will not come again,
And take from seventy springs a score,
It only leaves me fifty more.

And since to look at things in bloom
Fifty springs are little room,
About the woodlands I will go
To see the cherry hung with snow.

🕏 *From* Pippa Passes

Robert Browning 1812–1889

The year's at the spring,
And day's at the morn;
Morning's at seven;
The hillside's dew-pearled;
The lark's on the wing;
The snail's on the thorn;
God's in His Heaven –
All's right with the world!

❧ Gratitude

Edith Nesbit 1858–1924

I found a starving cat in the street:
It cried for food and a place by the fire.
I carried it home, and I strove to meet
The claims of its desire.

And since its desire was a little fish,
A little hay and a little milk,
I gave it cream in a silver dish
And a basket lined with silk.

And when we came to the grateful pause
When it should have fawned on the hand that fed,
It turned to a devil all teeth and claws,
Scratched me and bit me and fled.

To pay for the fish and the milk and the hay
With a purr had been an easy task:
But its hate and my blood were required to pay
For the gifts that it did not ask.

❧ May Night

Sara Teasdale 1884–1933

The spring is fresh and fearless
And every leaf is new,
The world is brimmed with moonlight,
The lilac brimmed with dew.

Here in the moving shadows
I catch my breath and sing –
My heart is fresh and fearless
And over-brimmed with spring.

❧ Today

Billy Collins 1941–

If ever there were a spring day so perfect,
so uplifted by a warm intermittent breeze

that it made you want to throw
open all the windows in the house

and unlatch the door to the canary's cage,
indeed, rip the little door from its jamb,

a day when the cool brick paths
and the garden bursting with peonies

seemed so etched in sunlight
that you felt like taking

a hammer to the glass paperweight
on the living room end table,

releasing the inhabitants
from their snow-covered cottage

so they could walk out,
holding hands and squinting

into this larger dome of blue and white,
well, today is just that kind of day.

Having a Coke with You

Frank O'Hara 1926–1966

is even more fun than going to San Sebastian, Irún,
    Hendaye, Biarritz, Bayonne
or being sick to my stomach on the Travesera de Gracia in
    Barcelona
partly because in your orange shirt you look like a better
    happier St. Sebastian
partly because of my love for you, partly because of your
    love for yoghurt
partly because of the fluorescent orange tulips around the
    birches
partly because of the secrecy our smiles take on before
    people and statuary
it is hard to believe when I'm with you that there can be
    anything as still
as solemn as unpleasantly definitive as statuary when right
    in front of it
in the warm New York 4 o'clock light we are drifting back
    and forth
between each other like a tree breathing through its
    spectacles

and the portrait show seems to have no faces in it at all,
    just paint
you suddenly wonder why in the world anyone ever did
    them

                  I look
at you and I would rather look at you than all the portraits
    in the world

except possibly for the *Polish Rider* occasionally and
   anyway it's in the Frick
which thank heavens you haven't gone to yet so we can go
   together for the first time
and the fact that you move so beautifully more or less
   takes care of Futurism
just as at home I never think of the *Nude Descending a
   Staircase* or
at a rehearsal a single drawing of Leonardo or
   Michelangelo that used to wow me
and what good does all the research of the Impressionists
   do them
when they never got the right person to stand near the tree
   when the sun sank
or for that matter Marino Marini when he didn't pick the
   rider as carefully
as the horse
                              it seems they were all
cheated of some marvelous experience
which is not going to go wasted on me which is why I'm
   telling you about it

❧ The Orange

Wendy Cope 1945–

At lunchtime I bought a huge orange –
The size of it made us all laugh.
I peeled it and shared it with Robert and Dave –
They got quarters and I had a half.

And that orange, it made me so happy,
As ordinary things often do
Just lately. The shopping. A walk in the park.
This is peace and contentment. It's new.

The rest of the day was quite easy.
I did all the jobs on my list
And enjoyed them and had some time over.
I love you. I'm glad I exist.

❧ The Guest House

Rumi 1207–1273
Translated by Coleman Barks

This being human is a guest house.
Every morning a new arrival.

A joy, a depression, a meanness,
some momentary awareness comes
as an unexpected visitor.

Welcome and entertain them all!
Even if they're a crowd of sorrows,
who violently sweep your house
empty of its furniture,
still, treat each guest honorably.
He may be clearing you out
for some new delight.

The dark thought, the shame, the malice,
meet them at the door laughing,
and invite them in.

Be grateful for whoever comes,
because each has been sent
as a guide from beyond.

❧ Desiderata

Max Ehrmann 1872–1945

Go placidly amid the noise and the haste,
and remember what peace there may be in silence.
As far as possible, without surrender,
be on good terms with all persons.
Speak your truth quietly and clearly;
and listen to others,
even to the dull and the ignorant;
they too have their story.
Avoid loud and aggressive persons;
they are vexatious to the spirit.
If you compare yourself with others,
you may become vain or bitter,
for always there will be greater and lesser persons than
    yourself.
Enjoy your achievements as well as your plans.
Keep interested in your own career, however humble;
it is a real possession in the changing fortunes of time.
Exercise caution in your business affairs,
for the world is full of trickery.
But let this not blind you to what virtue there is;
many persons strive for high ideals,
and everywhere life is full of heroism.
Be yourself.
Especially do not feign affection.
Neither be cynical about love;
for in the face of all aridity and disenchantment,
it is as perennial as the grass.
Take kindly the counsel of the years,
gracefully surrendering the things of youth.

Nurture strength of spirit to shield you in sudden
  misfortune.
But do not distress yourself with dark imaginings.
Many fears are born of fatigue and loneliness.
Beyond a wholesome discipline,
be gentle with yourself.
You are a child of the universe
no less than the trees and the stars;
you have a right to be here.
And whether or not it is clear to you,
no doubt the universe is unfolding as it should.
Therefore be at peace with God,
whatever you conceive Him to be.
And whatever your labors and aspirations,
in the noisy confusion of life, keep peace in your soul.
With all its sham, drudgery and broken dreams,
it is still a beautiful world.
Be cheerful.
Strive to be happy.

❧ May (from *The Shoemaker's Holiday*)

Thomas Dekker *c.* 1572–1632

O! the month of May, the merry month of May,
  So frolic, so gay, and so green, so green, so green!
O! and then did I unto my true Love say,
  Sweet Peg, thou shalt be my Summer's Queen.

Now the nightingale, the pretty nightingale,
  The sweetest singer in all the forest's choir,
Entreats thee, sweet Peggy, to hear thy true Love's tale:
  Lo! Yonder she sitteth, her breast against a briar.

But O! I spy the cuckoo, the cuckoo, the cuckoo;
  See where she sitteth; come away, my joy:
Come away, I prithee, I do not like the cuckoo
  Should sing where my Peggy and I kiss and toy,

O! the month of May, the merry month of May,
  So frolic, so gay, and so green, so green, so green!
And then did I unto my true Love say,
  Sweet Peg, thou shalt be my Summer's Queen.

❧ May Morning

John Milton 1608–1674

Now the bright morning Star, Dayes harbinger,
  Comes dancing from the East, and leads with her
  The Flowry May, who from her green lap throws
The yellow Cowslip, and the pale Primrose.
  Hail bounteous May that dost inspire
  Mirth and youth, and warm desire,
  Woods and Groves, are of thy dressing,
  Hill and Dale, doth boast thy blessing.
Thus we salute thee with our early Song,
And welcom thee, and wish thee long.

❧ The May Queen

Alfred, Lord Tennyson 1809–1892

You must wake and call me early, call me early, mother
  dear;
To-morrow 'ill be the happiest time of all the glad New-
  year;
Of all the glad New-year, mother, the maddest, merriest
  day;
For I'm to be Queen o' the May, mother, I'm to be
  Queen o' the May.

There's many a black, black eye, they say, but none so
  bright as mine;
There's Margaret and Mary, there's Kate and Caroline:
But none so fair as little Alice in all the land, they say,
So I'm to be Queen o' the May, mother, I'm to be Queen
  o' the May.

I sleep so sound all night, mother, that I shall never wake,
If you do not call me loud when the day begins to break:
But I must gather knots of flowers, and buds and garlands
  gay,
For I'm to be Queen o' the May, mother, I'm to be
  Queen o' the May.

As I came up the valley, whom think ye should I see,
But Robin leaning on the bridge beneath the hazel-tree?
He thought of that sharp look, mother, I gave him
  yesterday,—
But I'm to be Queen o' the May, mother, I'm to be
  Queen o' the May.

He thought I was a ghost, mother, for I was all in white,
And I ran by him without speaking, like a flash of light.
They call me cruel-hearted, but I care not what they say,
For I'm to be Queen o' the May, mother, I'm to be Queen
　　o' the May.

They say he's dying all for love, but that can never be;
They say his heart is breaking, mother—what is that to
　　me?
There's many a bolder lad 'ill woo me any summer day;
And I'm to be Queen o' the May, mother, I'm to be Queen
　　o' the May.

Little Effie shall go with me to-morrow to the green,
And you'll be there, too, mother, to see me made the
　　Queen;
For the shepherd lads on every side 'll come from far
　　away;
And I'm to be Queen o' the May, mother, I'm to be Queen
　　o' the May.

The honeysuckle round the porch has woven its wavy
　　bowers,
And by the meadow-trenches blow the faint sweet cuckoo-
　　flowers;
And the wild marsh-marigold shines like fire in swamps
　　and hollows gray,
And I'm to be Queen o' the May, mother, I'm to be Queen
　　o' the May.

The night-winds come and go, mother, upon the meadow-
   grass,
And the happy stars above them seem to brighten as they
   pass;
There will not be a drop of rain the whole of the livelong
   day,
And I'm to be Queen o' the May, mother, I'm to be Queen
   o' the May.

All the valley, mother, 'ill be fresh and green and still,
And the cowslip and the crowfoot are over all the hill,
And the rivulet in the flowery dale 'ill merrily glance and
   play,
For I'm to be Queen o' the May, mother, I'm to be Queen
   o' the May.

So you must wake and call me early, call me early, mother
   dear,
To-morrow 'ill be the happiest time of all the glad New-
   year:
To-morrow 'ill be of all the year the maddest, merriest
   day,
For I'm to be Queen o' the May, mother, I'm to be Queen
   o' the May.

❧ The Green Linnet

William Wordsworth 1770–1850

Beneath these fruit-tree boughs that shed
Their snow-white blossoms on my head,
With brightest sunshine round me spread
Of spring's unclouded weather,
In this sequestered nook how sweet
To sit upon my orchard-seat!
And birds and flowers once more to greet,
My last year's friends together.

One have I marked, the happiest guest
In all this covert of the blest:
Hail to Thee, far above the rest
In joy of voice and pinion!
Thou, Linnet! in thy green array,
Presiding Spirit here to-day,
Dost lead the revels of the May;
And this is thy dominion.

While birds, and butterflies, and flowers,
Make all one band of paramours,
Thou, ranging up and down the bowers,
Art sole in thy employment:
A Life, a Presence like the Air,
Scattering thy gladness without care,
Too blest with any one to pair;
Thyself thy own enjoyment.

Amid yon tuft of hazel trees,
That twinkle to the gusty breeze,
Behold him perched in ecstasies,
Yet seeming still to hover;
There! where the flutter of his wings
Upon his back and body flings
Shadows and sunny glimmerings,
That cover him all over.

My dazzled sight he oft deceives,
A brother of the dancing leaves;
Then flits, and from the cottage-eaves
Pours forth his song in gushes;
As if by that exulting strain
He mocked and treated with disdain
The voiceless Form he chose to feign,
While fluttering in the bushes.

❧ Prayer for Life (traditional Tewa prayer)

Anon

Our old women gods, we ask you!
Our old women gods, we ask you!
Then give us long life together,
May we live until our frosted hair is white;
May we live till then.
This life that now we know!

❧ Prayer to Mother Earth

Anon

Mother, may I value your gifts.
May humanity's care reach you and our gratitude
  rejuvenate you.
O Mother Earth, gently teach me to be a child worthy of
  your greatness.

❧ Great Spirit Prayer

Chief Yellow Lark *c.* 1850–1915

Oh, Great Spirit,
Whose voice I hear in the winds
and whose breath gives life to all the world.
Hear me! I need your strength and wisdom.
Let me walk in beauty, and make my eyes
ever hold the red and purple sunset.
Make my hands respect the things you have made
and my ears sharp to hear your voice.
Make me wise so that I may understand
the things you have taught my people.
Let me learn the lessons you have hidden
in every leaf and rock.

Help me remain calm and strong in the
face of all that comes towards me.
Help me find compassion without
empathy overwhelming me.
I seek strength, not to be greater than my brother,
but to fight my greatest enemy: myself.
Make me always ready to come to you
with clean hands and straight eyes.
So when life fades, as the fading sunset,
my spirit may come to you without shame.

❧ The Windhover

Gerard Manley Hopkins 1844–1889

I caught this morning morning's minion, king-
  dom of daylight's dauphin, dapple-dawn-drawn Falcon,
  in his riding
  Of the rolling level underneath him steady air, and
    striding
High there, how he rung upon the rein of a wimpling
  wing
In his ecstasy! then off, off forth on swing,
  As a skate's heel sweeps smooth on a bow-bend: the
    hurl and gliding
  Rebuffed the big wind. My heart in hiding
Stirred for a bird, – the achieve of, the mastery of the
  thing!

Brute beauty and valour and act, oh, air, pride, plume,
  here
  Buckle! AND the fire that breaks from thee then, a
    billion
Times told lovelier, more dangerous, O my chevalier!

  No wonder of it: shéer plód makes plough down sillion
Shine, and blue-bleak embers, ah my dear,
  Fall, gall themselves, and gash gold-vermilion.

❧ Sonnet 18

William Shakespeare 1564–1616

Shall I compare thee to a summer's day?
Thou art more lovely and more temperate:
Rough winds do shake the darling buds of May,
And summer's lease hath all too short a date;
Sometime too hot the eye of heaven shines,
And often is his gold complexion dimm'd;
And every fair from fair sometime declines,
By chance or nature's changing course untrimm'd;
But thy eternal summer shall not fade,
Nor lose possession of that fair thou ow'st;
Nor shall death brag thou wander'st in his shade,
When in eternal lines to time thou grow'st:
 So long as men can breathe or eyes can see,
 So long lives this, and this gives life to thee.

❧ *From* Auguries of Innocence

William Blake 1757–1827

To see a World in a Grain of Sand
And a Heaven in a Wild Flower
Hold Infinity in the palm of your hand
And Eternity in an hour

❧ Amazing Grace

John Newton 1725–1807

Amazing grace! (how sweet the sound!)
That sav'd a wretch like me!
I once was lost, but now am found;
Was blind, but now I see.

'Twas grace that taught my heart to fear,
And grace my fears reliev'd;
How precious did that grace appear,
The hour I first believ'd!

Thro' many dangers, toils, and snares,
I have already come;
'Tis grace that brought me safe thus far,
And grace will lead me home.

The Lord has promis'd good to me,
His word my hope secures;
He will my shield and portion be
As long as life endures.

Yes, when this flesh and heart shall fail,
And mortal life shall cease;
I shall possess, within the veil,
A life of joy and peace.

The earth shall soon dissolve like snow,
The sun forbear to shine;
But God, who call'd me here below,
Will be for ever mine.

❧ Serenity Prayer

Brian Bilston

Send me a slow news day,
a quiet, subdued day,
in which nothing much happens of note,
just the passing of time,
the consumption of wine,
and a re-run of *Murder, She Wrote*.

Grant me a no news day,
a spare-me-your-views day,
in which nothing much happens at all –
a few hours together,
some regional weather,
a day we can barely recall.

❧ On Work

Kahlil Gibran 1883–1931

Then a ploughman said, Speak to us of Work.
And he answered, saying:
You work that you may keep pace with the earth and the
soul of the earth.
For to be idle is to become a stranger unto the seasons,
and to step out of life's procession, that marches in
majesty and proud submission towards the infinite.

When you work you are a flute through whose heart the
whispering of the hours turns to music.
Which of you would be a reed, dumb and silent, when
all else sings together in unison?

Always you have been told that work is a curse and labour
a misfortune.
But I say to you that when you work you fulfil a part of
earth's furthest dream, assigned to you when the
dream was born,
And in keeping yourself with labour you are in truth
loving life,
And to love life through labour is to be intimate with life's
inmost secret.

But if you in your pain call birth an affliction and the
support of the flesh a curse written upon your brow,
then I answer that naught but the sweat of your brow
shall wash away that which is written.

You have been told also that life is darkness, and in your
    weariness you echo what was said by the weary.
And I say that life is indeed darkness save when there is
    urge,
And all urge is blind save when there is knowledge,
And all knowledge is vain save when there is work,
And all work is empty save when there is love;
And when you work with love you bind yourself to
    yourself, and to one another, and to God.

And what is it to work with love?
It is to weave the cloth with threads drawn from your
    heart, even as if your beloved were to wear that cloth.
It is to build a house with affection, even as if your
    beloved were to dwell in that house.
It is to sow seeds with tenderness and reap the harvest
    with joy, even as if your beloved were to eat the fruit.
It is to charge all things you fashion with a breath of your
    own spirit,
And to know that all the blessed dead are standing about
    you and watching.

Often have I heard you say, as if speaking in sleep, "He
    who works in marble, and finds the shape of his own
    soul in the stone, is nobler than he who ploughs the soil.
And he who seizes the rainbow to lay it on a cloth in the
    likeness of man, is more than he who makes the sandals
    for our feet."
But I say, not in sleep but in the overwakefulness of
    noontide, that the wind speaks not more sweetly to the
    giant oaks than to the least of all the blades of grass;
And he alone is great who turns the voice of the wind into
    a song made sweeter by his own loving.

Work is love made visible.

And if you cannot work with love but only with distaste, it is better that you should leave your work and sit at the gate of the temple and take alms of those who work with joy.

For if you bake bread with indifference, you bake a bitter bread that feeds but half man's hunger.

And if you grudge the crushing of the grapes, your grudge distils a poison in the wine.

And if you sing though as angels, and love not the singing, you muffle man's ears to the voices of the day and the voices of the night.

❧ Summer Rain

Amy Lowell 1874–1925

All night our room was outer-walled with rain.
Drops fell and flattened on the tin roof,
And rang like little disks of metal.
Ping!—Ping!—and there was not a pin-point of silence
    between
        them.
The rain rattled and clashed,
And the slats of the shutters danced and glittered.
But to me the darkness was red-gold and crocus-colored
With your brightness,
And the words you whispered to me
Sprang up and flamed—orange torches against the rain.
Torches against the wall of cool, silver rain!

❧ The Summer Day

Mary Oliver 1935–2019

Who made the world?
Who made the swan, and the black bear?
Who made the grasshopper?
This grasshopper, I mean—
the one who has flung herself out of the grass,
the one who is eating sugar out of my hand,
who is moving her jaws back and forth instead of up and
    down—
who is gazing around with her enormous and complicated
    eyes.
Now she lifts her pale forearms and thoroughly washes her
    face.
Now she snaps her wings open, and floats away.
I don't know exactly what a prayer is.
I do know how to pay attention, how to fall down
into the grass, how to kneel down in the grass,
how to be idle and blessed, how to stroll through the
    fields,
which is what I have been doing all day.
Tell me, what else should I have done?
Doesn't everything die at last, and too soon?
Tell me, what is it you plan to do
with your one wild and precious life?

June

Joy

A

S we approach the summer equinox, the natural world is at its prime in June, with trees, plants and flowers in full bloom. The month is named after Juno, the queen of the Roman gods, evoking her association with the twin beauties of summer and youth; it is a time for celebrating joy in its many different forms. Whether reflecting the pleasure of human connection or observing the splendour of the Earth, joy is a theme that poets thankfully return to often. As the great Romantic poet John Keats wrote, 'A thing of beauty is a joy forever'. Each poem collected in this month crystallises a flash of beauty or joy, guaranteeing Keats' promise that 'it will never / Pass into nothingness.'

The flourishing of flora and fauna at the height of summer has long given poets cause to express their joy, but poetry is perhaps at its finest when it is able to represent that which is intangible; birdsong, movement, the rush of the wind. The contemporary Welsh poet Gillian Clarke's 'Ode to Joy' ushers in the month with a 'Salutation/ to long midsummer days'. Clarke's sky becomes a 'theatre of summer', brimming with bats 'scribbling verse on twilight' and singing birds; it is as though the whole of nature simply performs for our delight.

Poetry in praise of birdsong often emulates its twittering gleefulness, as with the anonymous Middle English poem 'Sumer is i-cumin in' and its varied refrain of 'sing, cuccu'; especially with the distance of time making its language less familiar, this poem in particular has its primary virtue in sound, not sense. Percy Bysshe Shelley's breathless ode 'To a Skylark' is a loftier representation, but operates along similar lines; 'Higher still and higher/ From the earth thou springest/ Like a cloud of fire;/ The blue deep thou wingest,/ And singing still dost soar, and soaring ever singest.' The contemporary poet and human rights activist Rose Styron's understated, untitled work provides the mirror image of this technique, with her brief, laconic lines infused with the quiet peace she represents: 'No one's awake/ but us, and a bird.'

This month is full of powerful female poets, including 'Michael Field', the pseudonym shared by the Victorian lovers and collaborators Katherine Harris Bradley and Edith Emma Cooper. And it is a particular joy to include a poem by Clarissa Scott Delany, a poet from the 1920s revival of African-American culture in New York known as the Harlem Renaissance. Delany's lucid opening verse emphasises the connection between nature and joy. Her description of joy shaking her 'Like the roistering wind / That laughs through the stalwart pines' highlights the multidirectional resemblance between the movement of joy and that of the wind. Delany's rollocking succession of ideas also 'floods' the reader's mind like flashes of sun on 'rain-drenched trees', the poem masterfully uniting content and form.

But of course, there are countless other sorts of joy, recounted by writers from the Bengali polymath Rabindranath Tagore to the award-winning contemporary poet Ocean Vuong. Even the Buddhist Canon demands our attention this month, with plain-speaking reminders to 'live in joy, not hating those who hate us' and that 'craving is the worst disease.' And for all the different types of joy, poets find unique modes of expression. There is comedy in Rudyard Kipling's humorous ode to the pleasure of 'a well-made Lie'. Kipling's poem becomes its own boisterous expression of the lengths to which a metaphor might extend, taking pleasure in the silliness and snobbery of its own internal rhymes: 'Not a little-place-at-Tooting, but a country-house-with-shooting/ And a ring-fence-deer-park Lie.' And on the other end of the spectrum there is the earnest, ecstatic anatomy of Walt Whitman's 'I Sing the Body Electric'. 'Leg-fibres, knee, knee-pan, upper-leg, underleg' – nothing lies below the scope of Whitman's view.

The joyful month of June concludes with one of the most recent poems in this book, by the award-winning Californian poet and essayist Danusha Laméris. Laméris highlights the joy of small kindnesses, asking: 'What if they are the true dwelling of the holy, these/ fleeting temples we make together when we say, 'Here,/ have my seat,' 'Go ahead – you first,' 'I like your hat.' It is a message to take away not just for the summer, but to carry through the whole year. Her emphasis on the importance of the simple things in an age 'So far/ from tribe and fire' calls to mind Toni Morrison's suggestion that fundamentally 'finding, incorporating and then representing beauty is what humans do': 'This overwhelming beauty – some of it is natural, some of it is man-made, some of it is casual, some of it is a mere glance – it is an absolute necessity. I don't think we can do without it any more than we can do without dreams or oxygen.'

Even after all this time
the sun never says to the earth,
'You owe me.'

Look what happens with
a love like that,
it lights the whole sky.

Hafez

❧ Ode to Joy

Gillian Clarke 1937–

Exultation! Salutation
to the long midsummer days,
to the light lost by the minute,
sing, and sing the dark away.

In the park the lovers listen,
blackbird's last song of the day.
Bats are scribbling verse on twilight.
Owls are calling, Kyrie.

Soon a gathering of swallows,
like a stanza on a wire,
voices rising in crescendo,
in hall and stadium and choir.

In the theatre of summer
stars ascending in their arc,
company and conversation.
Sing, and sing away the dark!

❧ Eternity

William Blake 1757–1827

He who binds to himself a joy
Does the winged life destroy
He who kisses the joy as it flies
Lives in eternity's sunrise

ॐ Joy

Clarissa Scott Delany 1901–1927

Joy shakes me like the wind that lifts a sail,
Like the roistering wind
That laughs through stalwart pines.
It floods me like the sun
On rain-drenched trees
That flash with silver and green.

I abandon myself to joy—
I laugh—I sing.
Too long have I walked a desolate way,
Too long stumbled down a maze
Bewildered.

❧ On Joy and Sorrow

Kahlil Gibran 1883–1931

Then a woman said, Speak to us of Joy and Sorrow.

And he answered:

Your joy is your sorrow unmasked.

And the selfsame well from which your laughter rises was
oftentimes filled with your tears.

And how else can it be?

The deeper that sorrow carves into your being, the more
joy you can contain.

Is not the cup that holds your wine the very cup that was
burned in the potter's oven?

And is not the lute that soothes your spirit, the very wood
that was hollowed with knives?

When you are joyous, look deep into your heart and you
shall find it is only that which has given you sorrow that
is giving you joy.

When you are sorrowful look again in your heart, and you
shall see that in truth you are weeping for that which
has been your delight.

Some of you say, "Joy is greater than sorrow," and others
say, "Nay, sorrow is the greater."

But I say unto you, they are inseparable.

Together they come, and when one sits alone with you at
your board, remember that the other is asleep upon
your bed.

Verily you are suspended like scales between your sorrow
and your joy.
Only when you are empty are you at standstill and
balanced.
When the treasure-keeper lifts you to weigh his gold and
his silver, needs must your joy or your sorrow rise or
fall.

❧ In the Mountains on a Summer Day

Li Po 701 AD–762 AD

Gently I stir a white feather fan,
With open shirt sitting in a green wood.
I take off my cap and hang it on a jutting stone;
A wind from the pine-trees trickles on my bare head.

❧ There is pleasure in the wet wet clay

Rudyard Kipling 1865–1936

There is pleasure in the wet wet clay,
When the artist's hand is potting it.
There is pleasure in the wet wet lay,
When the poet's pad is blotting it.
There is pleasure in the shine of your picture on the line
At the Royal Acade-my;
But the pleasure felt in these, is as chalk to Cheddar
   cheese
When it comes to a well-made Lie.
To a quite unwreckable Lie
To a most impeccable Lie!
To a water-tight, fire-proof, angle-iron, sunk-hinge, time-
   lock, steel-faced Lie!
Not a private hansom Lie
But a pair-and-brougham Lie
Not a little-place-at-Tooting, but a country-house-with-
   shooting
And a ring-fence, deer-park Lie.

❧ A Moment

Mary Elizabeth Coleridge 1861–1907

The clouds had made a crimson crown
Above the mountains high.
The stormy sun was going down
In a stormy sky.

Why did you let your eyes so rest on me,
And hold your breath between?
In all the ages this can never be
As if it had not been.

🐦 On Earth We're Briefly Gorgeous

Ocean Vuong 1988–

i

Tell me it was for the hunger
& nothing less. For hunger is to give
the body what it knows

it cannot keep. That this amber light
whittled down by another war
is all that pins my hand

to your chest.

i

You, drowning
    between my arms —
stay.

You, pushing your body
    into the river
only to be left
    with yourself —
stay.

i

I'll tell you how we're wrong enough to be forgiven. How
    one night, after
backhanding
mother, then taking a chainsaw to the kitchen table, my
    father went to kneel
in the bathroom until we heard his muffled cries through
    the walls.
And so I learned that a man, in climax, was the closest
    thing
to surrender.

i

Say surrender. Say alabaster. Switchblade.
    Honeysuckle. Goldenrod. Say autumn.
Say autumn despite the green
    in your eyes. Beauty despite
daylight. Say you'd kill for it. Unbreakable dawn
    mounting in your throat.
My thrashing beneath you
    like a sparrow stunned
with falling.

i

Dusk: a blade of honey between our shadows, draining.

i

I wanted to disappear—so I opened the door to a stranger's
car. He was divorced. He was still alive. He was sobbing into
his hands (hands that tasted like rust). The pink breast cancer
ribbon on his keychain swayed in the ignition. Don't we touch
each other just to prove we are still here? I was still here once.
The moon, distant & flickering, trapped itself in beads of sweat
on my neck. I let the fog spill through the cracked window &

cover my fangs. When I left, the Buick kept sitting there, a dumb bull in pasture, its eyes searing my shadow onto the side of suburban houses. At home, I threw myself on the bed like a torch & watched the flames gnaw through my mother's house until the sky appeared, bloodshot & massive. How I wanted to be that sky—to hold every flying & falling at once.

i

Say amen. Say amend.

Say yes. Say yes

anyway.

i

In the shower, sweating under cold water, I scrubbed & scrubbed.

i

In the life before this one, you could tell
two people were in love
because when they drove the pickup
over the bridge, their wings
would grow back just in time.

Some days I am still inside the pickup.
Some days I keep waiting.

i

It's not too late. Our heads haloed
   with gnats & summer too early
to leave any marks.
   Your hand under my shirt as static
intensifies on the radio.
   Your other hand pointing
your daddy's revolver
   to the sky. Stars falling one
by one in the cross hairs.
   This means I won't be
afraid if we're already
   here. Already more
than skin can hold. That a body
   beside a body
must make a field
   full of ticking. That your name
is only the sound of clocks
   being set back another hour
& morning
   finds our clothes
on your mother's front porch, shed
   like week-old lilies.

✇ Beauty

Edward Thomas 1878–1917

What does it mean? Tired, angry, and ill at ease,
No man, woman, or child alive could please
Me now. And yet I almost dare to laugh
Because I sit and frame an epitaph—
'Here lies all that no one loved of him
And that loved no one.' Then in a trice that whim
Has wearied. But, though I am like a river
At fall of evening while it seems that never
Has the sun lighted it or warmed it, while
Cross breezes cut the surface to a file,
This heart, some fraction of me, happily
Floats through the window even now to a tree
Down in the misting, dim-lit, quiet vale,
Not like a pewit that returns to wail
For something it has lost, but like a dove
That slants unswerving to its home and love.
There I find my rest, as through the dusk air
Flies what yet lives in me: Beauty is there.

❧ The Swing

Robert Louis Stevenson 1850–1894

How do you like to go up in a swing,
　Up in the air so blue?
Oh, I do think it the pleasantest thing
　Ever a child can do!

Up in the air and over the wall,
　Till I can see so wide,
Rivers and trees and cattle and all
　Over the countryside—

Till I look down on the garden green,
　Down on the roof so brown—
Up in the air I go flying again,　.
　Up in the air and down!

❧ Sumer is i-cumin in

Anon

Sing, cuccu, nu. Sing, cuccu.
Sing, cuccu. Sing, cuccu, nu.

Sumer is i-cumin in—
Lhude sing, cuccu!
Groweth sed and bloweth med
And springth the wude nu.
Sing, cuccu!

Awe bleteth after lomb,
Lhouth after calve cu,
Bulluc sterteth, bucke verteth—
Murie sing, cuccu!
Cuccu, cuccu,
Wel singes thu, cuccu.
Ne swik thu naver nu!

❧ Summer

John Clare 1793–1864

Come we to the summer, to the summer we will come,
For the woods are full of bluebells and the hedges full of
 bloom,
And the crow is on the oak a-building of her nest,
And love is burning diamonds in my true lover's breast;
She sits beneath the whitethorn a-plaiting of her hair,
And I will to my true lover with a fond request repair;
I will look upon her face, I will in her beauty rest,
And lay my aching weariness upon her lovely breast.

The clock-a-clay is creeping on the open bloom of May,
The merry bee is trampling the pinky threads all day,
And the chaffinch it is brooding on its grey mossy nest
In the whitethorn bush where I will lean upon my lover's
 breast;
I'll lean upon her breast and I'll whisper in her ear
That I cannot get a wink o'sleep for thinking of my dear;
I hunger at my meat and I daily fade away
Like the hedge rose that is broken in the heat of the day.

❧ A Summer Wind

Michael Field 1846–1914, 1862–1913

O wind, thou hast thy kingdom in the trees,
  And all thy royalties
  Sweep through the land to-day.
    It is mid June,
And thou, with all thy instruments in tune,
  Thine orchestra
Of heaving fields and heavy swinging fir,
    Strikest a lay
    That doth rehearse
Her ancient freedom to the universe.
  All other sound in awe
    Repeats its law:
  The bird is mute; the sea
  Sucks up its waves; from rain
  The burthened clouds refrain,
To listen to thee in thy leafery,
    Thou unconfined,
Lavish, large, soothing, refluent summer wind.

❧ *From* Thyrsis: A Monody

Matthew Arnold 1822–1888

Too quick despairer, wherefore wilt thou go?
Soon will the high Midsummer pomps come on,
Soon will the musk carnations break and swell,
Soon shall we have gold-dusted snapdragon,
Sweet-William with his homely cottage-smell,
And stocks in fragrant blow;
Roses that down the alleys shine afar,
And open, jasmine-muffled lattices,
And groups under the dreaming garden-trees,
And the full moon, and the white evening-star.

🐦 Wild Mountain Thyme (Folk Song)

Anon

O the summer time is coming and the trees are sweetly
  blooming
And the wild mountain thyme grows around the purple heather.
  Will you go, lassie go and we'll all go together
  To pluck wild mountain thyme around the blooming
    heather
  Will you go lassie go?

I will build my love a bower by yon crystal flowing fountain
And on it I will pile all the flowers of the mountain
  Will you go, lassie go and we'll all go together
  To pluck wild mountain thyme around the blooming
    heather
  Will you go lassie go?

If my true love will not go, I can surely find another
Where the wild mountain thyme grows around the purple
  heather
  Will you go, lassie go and we'll all go together
  To pluck wild mountain thyme around the blooming
    heather
  Will you go lassie go?

I will build my love a shelter on yon high mountain green
And my love shall be the fairest that the summer sun has seen
  Will you go, lassie go and we'll all go together
  To pluck wild mountain thyme around the blooming
    heather
  Will you go lassie go?

❧ The unknown bird

Edward Thomas 1878–1917

Three lovely notes he whistled, too soft to be heard
If others sang; but others never sang
In the great beech-wood all that May and June.
No one saw him: I alone could hear him
Though many listened. Was it but four years
Ago? or five? He never came again.

Oftenest when I heard him I was alone,
Nor could I ever make another hear.
La-la-la! he called, seeming far-off—
As if a cock crowed past the edge of the world,
As if the bird or I were in a dream.
Yet that he travelled through the trees and sometimes
Neared me, was plain, though somehow distant still
He sounded. All the proof is—I told men
What I had heard.

I never knew a voice,
Man, beast, or bird, better than this. I told
The naturalists; but neither had they heard
Anything like the notes that did so haunt me,
I had them clear by heart and have them still.
Four years, or five, have made no difference. Then
As now that La-la-la! was bodiless sweet:
Sad more than joyful it was, if I must say
That it was one or other, but if sad
'Twas sad only with joy too, too far off
For me to taste it. But I cannot tell
If truly never anything but fair
The days were when he sang, as now they seem.
This surely I know, that I who listened then,
Happy sometimes, sometimes suffering
A heavy body and a heavy heart,
Now straightway, if I think of it, become
Light as that bird wandering beyond my shore.

❧ Untitled [No one's awake]

Rose Styron 1924–

No one's awake
but us, and a bird.
The day's too beautiful
to speak a word.

❧ Misty Rain

Matsuo Bashō 1644–1694
Translated by Robert Hass

Misty rain,
Mount Fuji is unseen for the day:
Enchanting!

❧ For keeps

Joy Harjo 1951–

Sun makes the day new.
Tiny green plants emerge from earth.
Birds are singing the sky into place.
There is nowhere else I want to be but here.
I lean into the rhythm of your heart to see where it will
    take us.
We gallop into a warm, southern wind.
I link my legs to yours and we ride together,
Toward the ancient encampment of our relatives.
Where have you been? they ask.
And what has taken you so long?
That night after eating, singing, and dancing
We lay together under the stars.
We know ourselves to be part of mystery.
It is unspeakable.
It is everlasting.
It is for keeps.

MARCH 4, 2013, CHAMPAIGN, ILLINOIS

❧ To a Skylark

Percy Bysshe Shelley 1792–1822

Hail to thee, blithe Spirit!
Bird thou never wert,
That from Heaven, or near it,
Pourest thy full heart
In profuse strains of unpremeditated art.

Higher still and higher
From the earth thou springest
Like a cloud of fire;
The blue deep thou wingest,
And singing still dost soar, and soaring ever singest.

In the golden lightning
Of the sunken sun,
O'er which clouds are bright'ning,
Thou dost float and run;
Like an unbodied joy whose race is just begun.

The pale purple even
Melts around thy flight;
Like a star of Heaven,
In the broad day-light
Thou art unseen, but yet I hear thy shrill delight,

Keen as are the arrows
Of that silver sphere,
Whose intense lamp narrows
In the white dawn clear
Until we hardly see, we feel that it is there.

All the earth and air
With thy voice is loud,
As, when night is bare,
From one lonely cloud
The moon rains out her beams, and Heaven is overflow'd.

What thou art we know not;
What is most like thee?
From rainbow clouds there flow not
Drops so bright to see
As from thy presence showers a rain of melody.

Like a Poet hidden
In the light of thought,
Singing hymns unbidden,
Till the world is wrought
To sympathy with hopes and fears it heeded not:

Like a high-born maiden
In a palace-tower,
Soothing her love-laden
Soul in secret hour
With music sweet as love, which overflows her bower:

Like a glow-worm golden
In a dell of dew,
Scattering unbeholden
Its aëreal hue
Among the flowers and grass, which screen it from the view:

Like a rose embower'd
In its own green leaves,
By warm winds deflower'd,
Till the scent it gives
Makes faint with too much sweet those heavy-winged thieves:

Sound of vernal showers
On the twinkling grass,
Rain-awaken'd flowers,
All that ever was
Joyous, and clear, and fresh, thy music doth surpass.

Teach us, Sprite or Bird,
What sweet thoughts are thine:
I have never heard
Praise of love or wine
That panted forth a flood of rapture so divine.

Chorus Hymeneal,
Or triumphal chant,
Match'd with thine would be all
But an empty vaunt,
A thing wherein we feel there is some hidden want.

What objects are the fountains
Of thy happy strain?
What fields, or waves, or mountains?
What shapes of sky or plain?
What love of thine own kind? what ignorance of pain?

With thy clear keen joyance
Languor cannot be:
Shadow of annoyance
Never came near thee:
Thou lovest: but ne'er knew love's sad satiety.

Waking or asleep,
Thou of death must deem
Things more true and deep
Than we mortals dream,
Or how could thy notes flow in such a crystal stream?

We look before and after,
And pine for what is not:
Our sincerest laughter
With some pain is fraught;
Our sweetest songs are those that tell of saddest thought.

Yet if we could scorn
Hate, and pride, and fear;
If we were things born
Not to shed a tear,
I know not how thy joy we ever should come near.

Better than all measures
Of delightful sound,
Better than all treasures
That in books are found,
Thy skill to poet were, thou scorner of the ground!

Teach me half the gladness
That thy brain must know,
Such harmonious madness
From my lips would flow
The world should listen then, as I am listening now.

❧ Happy the Man
(*from* Horace Ode 29, Book 3)

John Dryden 1631–1700

Happy the Man, and happy he alone,
  He, who can call today his own:
  He, who secure within, can say
Tomorrow do thy worst, for I have liv'd today.
  Be fair, or foul, or rain, or shine,
The joys I have possest, in spight of fate are mine
  Not Heav'n itself upon the past has pow'r;
But what has been, has been, and I have had my hour.

❧ From *Henry VI* (Part 3, Act 2, Scene 5)

William Shakespeare 1564–1616

O God! Methinks it were a happy life,
To be no better than a homely swain,
To sit upon a hill, as I do now,
To carve out dials quaintly, point by point,
Thereby to see the minutes how they run:
How many make the hour full complete,
How many hours bring about the day,
How many days will finish up the year,
How many years a mortal man may live.
When this is known, then to divide the times:
So many hours must I tend my flock,
So many hours must I take my rest,
So many hours must I contemplate,
So many hours must I sport myself,
So many days my ewes have been with young,
So many weeks ere the poor fools will ean,
So many years ere I shall shear the fleece.
So minutes, hours, days, months, and years,
Passed over to the end they were created,
Would bring white hairs unto a quiet grave.
Ah, what a life were this! How sweet! How lovely!

❧ The Sun Never Says

Hafez 1325–1390

Even after all this time
the sun never says to the earth,
'You owe me.'

Look what happens with
a love like that,
it lights the whole sky.

❧ *From* Endymion

John Keats 1795–1821

A thing of beauty is a joy for ever:
Its loveliness increases; it will never
Pass into nothingness; but still will keep
A bower quiet for us, and a sleep
Full of sweet dreams, and health, and quiet breathing.

❧ Light

Rabindranath Tagore 1861–1941

Light, my light, the world-filling light,
the eye-kissing light,
heart-sweetening light!

Ah, the light dances, my darling, at the center of my life;
the light strikes, my darling, the chords of my love;
the sky opens, the wind runs wild, laughter passes over the
earth.

The butterflies spread their sails on the sea of light.
Lilies and jasmines surge up on the crest of the waves of
light.

The light is shattered into gold on every cloud, my
darling,
and it scatters gems in profusion.

Mirth spreads from leaf to leaf, my darling,
and gladness without measure.
The heaven's river has drowned its banks
and the flood of joy is abroad.

❧ Happiness

Raymond Carver 1938–1988

So early it's still almost dark out.
I'm near the window with coffee,
and the usual early morning stuff
that passes for thought.
When I see the boy and his friend
walking up the road
to deliver the newspaper.
They wear caps and sweaters,
and one boy has a bag over his shoulder.
They are so happy
they aren't saying anything, these boys.
I think if they could, they would take
each other's arm.
It's early in the morning,
and they are doing this thing together.
They come on, slowly.
The sky is taking on light,
though the moon still hangs pale over the water.
Such beauty that for a minute
death and ambition, even love,
doesn't enter into this.
Happiness. It comes on
unexpectedly. And goes beyond, really,
any early morning talk about it.

❧ Adelstrop

Edward Thomas 1878–1917

Yes. I remember Adlestrop—
The name, because one afternoon
Of heat the express-train drew up there
Unwontedly. It was late June.

The steam hissed. Someone cleared his throat.
No one left and no one came
On the bare platform. What I saw
Was Adlestrop—only the name

And willows, willow-herb, and grass,
And meadowsweet, and haycocks dry,
No whit less still and lonely fair
Than the high cloudlets in the sky.

And for that minute a blackbird sang
Close by, and round him, mistier,
Farther and farther, all the birds
Of Oxfordshire and Gloucestershire.

Joy

Gautama Buddha 564 BC–?

Let us live in joy, not hating those who hate us.
Among those who hate us, we live free of hate.
Let us live in joy,
free from disease among those who are diseased.
Among those who are diseased, let us live free of disease.
Let us live in joy, free from greed among the greedy.
Among those who are greedy, we live free of greed.
Let us live in joy, though we possess nothing.
Let us live feeding on joy, like the bright gods.

Victory breeds hate, for the conquered is unhappy.
Whoever has given up victory and defeat
is content and lives joyfully.

There is no fire like lust, no misfortune like hate;
there is no pain like this body;
there is no joy higher than peace.

Craving is the worst disease;
disharmony is the greatest sorrow.
The one who knows this truly
knows that nirvana is the highest bliss.

Health is the greatest gift;
contentment is the greatest wealth;
trusting is the best relationship;
nirvana is the highest joy.

Whoever has tasted the sweetness
of solitude and tranquillity
becomes free from fear and sin
while drinking the sweetness of the truth.
The sight of the noble is good;
to live with them is always joyful.

Whoever does not see fools will always be happy.
Whoever associates with fools suffers a long time.
Being with fools, as with an enemy, is always painful.

Being with the wise, like meeting with family, is joyful.
Therefore, one should follow the wise, the intelligent,
the learned, the patient, the dutiful, the noble;
one should follow the good and wise,
as the moon follows the path of the stars.

❧ I Sing the Body Electric

Walt Whitman 1819–1892

O my body! I dare not desert the likes of you in other men
    and women, nor the likes of the parts of you,
I believe the likes of you are to stand or fall with the likes
    of the soul, (and that they are the soul,)
I believe the likes of you shall stand or fall with my
    poems, and that they are poems,
Man's, woman's, child's, youth's, wife's, husband's,
    mother's, father's, young man's, young woman's poems;
Head, neck, hair, ears, drop and tympan of the ears,
Eyes, eye-fringes, iris of the eye, eye-brows, and the
    waking or sleeping of the lids,
Mouth, tongue, lips, teeth, roof of the mouth, jaws, and
    the jaw-hinges,
Nose, nostrils of the nose, and the partition,
Cheeks, temples, forehead, chin, throat, back of the neck,
    neck-slue,
Strong shoulders, manly beard, scapula, hind-shoulders,
    and the ample side-round of the chest,
Upper-arm, arm-pit, elbow-socket, lower-arm, arm-
    sinews, arm-bones,
Wrist and wrist-joints, hand, palm, knuckles, thumb, fore-
    finger, finger-balls, finger-joints, finger-nails,
Broad breast-front, curling hair of the breast, breast-bone,
    breast-side,
Ribs, belly, backbone, joints of the backbone,
Hips, hip-sockets, hip-strength, inward and outward
    round, man-balls, man-root,
Strong set of thighs, well carrying the trunk above,
Leg fibres, knee, knee-pan, upper-leg, under leg,

Ankles, instep, foot-ball, toes, toe-joints, the heel;
All attitudes, all the shapeliness, all the belongings of my
    or your body, or of any one's body, male or female,
The lung-sponges, the stomach-sac, the bowels sweet and
    clean,
The brain in its folds inside the skull-frame,
Sympathies, heart-valves, palate-valves, sexuality,
    maternity,
Womanhood, and all that is a woman, and the man that
    comes from woman,
The womb, the teats, nipples, breast-milk, tears, laughter,
    weeping, love-looks, love-perturbations and risings,
The voice, articulation, language, whispering, shouting
    aloud,
Food, drink, pulse, digestion, sweat, sleep, walking,
    swimming,
Poise on the hips, leaping, reclining, embracing, arm-
    curving and tightening,
The continual changes of the flex of the mouth, and
    around the eyes,
The skin, the sunburnt shade, freckles, hair,
The curious sympathy one feels, when feeling with the
    hand the naked meat of the body,
The circling rivers, the breath, and breathing it in and out,
The beauty of the waist, and thence of the hips, and
    thence downward toward the knees,
The thin red jellies within you, or within me, the bones,
    and the marrow in the bones,
The exquisite realization of health;
O I say these are not the parts and poems of the body
    only, but of the soul,
O I say now these are the soul!

❧ Small Kindnesses

Danusha Laméris 1971–

I've been thinking about the way, when you walk
down a crowded aisle, people pull in their legs
to let you by. Or how strangers still say "bless you"
when someone sneezes, a leftover
from the Bubonic plague. "Don't die," we are saying.
And sometimes, when you spill lemons
from your grocery bag, someone else will help you
pick them up. Mostly, we don't want to harm each other.
We want to be handed our cup of coffee hot,
and to say thank you to the person handing it. To smile
at them and for them to smile back. For the waitress
to call us honey when she sets down the bowl of clam
    chowder,
and for the driver in the red pick-up truck to let us pass.
We have so little of each other, now. So far
from tribe and fire. Only these brief moments of exchange.
What if they are the true dwelling of the holy, these
fleeting temples we make together when we say, "Here,
have my seat," "Go ahead—you first," "I like your hat."

July

Escape

I F July is the month of escape, poetry is its language. When we're feeling trapped by the monotony of daily life, pining for the long summer breaks of our schooldays, or struggling to shake off a black mood, poems can send us on distant adventures and transport us to new states of mind. The poems collected for this month showcase a multitude of ways in which poetry offers release and unburdens us: by letting us explore different cultural movements and ways of life; by guiding us on imaginative journeys; and more generally by allowing us to escape the prosaic rhythm of everyday life. For as the French poet and essayist Paul Valéry once said, 'if prose is walking, poetry is dancing.'

It has often been said that Ireland has all the best poets, which perhaps explains why they have never settled on a national poet. Were they to do so, W.B. Yeats would certainly be a strong contender, as his works in this month make clear. 'The Lake Isle of Innisfree', one of his greatest poems, even had its first lines printed in the Irish passport: 'I will arise and go now, and go to Innisfree,/ And a small cabin build there, of clay and wattles made'. From the alluring Innisfree of Yeats' Irish childhood to the homely Chinese 'River Village' that Tu Fu charmingly describes, poetry always has somewhere to take us.

It should come as no surprise, then, that some of the month's crowning works are the ones that take us the furthest from our daily drudgery, such as John Gillespie Magee Jr.'s 'High Flight', an ecstatic description of flying. He wrote the poem for his parents while training as a pilot, and his enthusiasm is palpable: 'I have slipped the surly bonds of Earth/ And danced the skies on laughter-silvered wings;/ Sunward I've climbed, and joined the tumbling mirth/ of sun-split clouds, – and done a hundred things/ You have not dreamed of.' Even his surroundings cannot help but be intoxicated with his 'mirth'. But in the poignant way that poems can take on lives of their own and 'escape' from their original context, this poem gained another meaning when his parents published it in the wake of his death in a flying accident; escaping the Earth's 'surly bonds' to touch 'the face of God' suddenly takes on an entirely new sense of embracing one's death.

But sometimes the journeys are merely imaginative. Poetry can take us to whole new worlds, if only for a while . . . In 'Eldorado' Edgar Allan Poe tells the story of a quest to find the legendary city of gold, the eponymous Eldorado. The poem's repetition and rhythm create a lulling momentum that pulls us along with the knight on his journey, and though we never arrive anywhere it is surely a successful diversion. Similarly, Edward Lear's 'The Owl and the Pussy-Cat', which has delighted readers for generations, transports us to the dreamscapes of our childhood 'in a beautiful pea-green boat'. Lear's nonsense makes the clear point that poetry's gift lies not only in its sense but also in its sound.

Both Yeats' and Tu Fu's poems show yet another aspect of poetry's escapist power; its ability to draw together disparate cultures and milieus. The extraordinary appeal of Tu Fu's poetry, well over a thousand years after it was written, is partly explained by the way his writing fuses the traditions of China's two native religions, Confucianism and Daoism. In 'The River Village' he, like the river, 'encircles the village' until he enters his own home, looking at his 'old wife' and 'little sons', and eventually his own body ('I have many illnesses'), highlighting the unity between all creation, whether natural or manmade. It was written during a time in Tu Fu's life known as his 'thatched cottage' period, when he escaped from urban life by building a thatched cottage and spent four years ensconced in the countryside. Many consider it to be the peak of his creative output, as in these four years he wrote 240 poems. The thatched cottage still stands and attracts visitors to this day.

Yeats, for his part, was a central figure of the Celtic Revival, and poems such as 'The Lake Isle of Innisfree' manifest an Irish tradition which is distinct from English literature. Other traditions that find a place in this month's poems include Japan's haiku, with masterful works by Kobayashi Issa and Matsuo Bashō. Both highlight how grounding ourselves in the present moment, or what is known as mindfulness, can itself be a form of escape from the high-paced bustle of everyday life.

But verse's liberating power is perhaps never better highlighted than in the African American spiritual tradition, which crops up towards the end of the month with 'Swing Low, Sweet Chariot'. Although in Britain it is primarily known today as a rugby song, it was in fact written by Wallace Willis, a man who had been enslaved in America in the mid-nineteenth century, and its initial popularity was amongst other formerly enslaved people. Its lines, 'If you get there before I do [. . .] Tell all my friends I'm coming too' have led some to speculate that it might have been a reference to – or even used in – the Underground Railroad. But whether or not this is true, the song (and indeed the spiritual tradition altogether) remains a testament to poetry's power to bolster the indomitable human spirit, in even the darkest of times.

Enjoying a poem is one of the best ways to escape from the busyness of everyday life. But the poems are an escape for their authors too. Many of these works are by voices escaping their dominant genre. The early twentieth-century writer and publisher Virginia Woolf is best known for her incisive prose, in novels and essays such as *A Room of One's Own*. Here, she carves out a space for herself as a poet, using the rhythm and rhyme or verse to convey the relentless enthusiasm that summer's onset brings; 'Let us go, then, exploring/ This Summer morning,/ When all are adoring/ The plum blossom and the bee.' Another example is the Scottish children's writer, Robert Louis Stevenson. Though best known for his worldly adventure novels, such as *Treasure Island* and *Kidnapped*, here he represents escape as a domestic scene, with a child avoiding bedtime to gaze up at the stars: 'They saw me at last, and they chased me with cries,/ And then soon had me packed into bed;/ But the glory kept shining and bright in my eyes,/ And the stars going round in my head.' Once a marvellous vision or a glimpse of the stars has been imprinted on a child's mind, it stays there; why else does Yeats return to Innisfree? Especially in the context of Stevenson's ill health causing him to spend much of his life confined indoors, the notion that our memories can be a mode of escape is a powerful one and is reinforced through remembering verse. As Yeats says of the lapping water of Innisfree: 'While I stand on the roadway, or on the pavements grey, / I hear it in the deep heart's core.'

Afoot and light-hearted I
take to the open road,
Healthy, free, the world before me,
The long brown path before me
leading wherever I choose.

Walt Whitman

❧ What If This Road

Sheenagh Pugh 1950–

What if this road, that has held no surprises
these many years, decided not to go
home after all; what if it could turn
left or right with no more ado
than a kite-tail? What if its tarry skin
were like a long, supple bolt of cloth,
that is shaken and rolled out, and takes
a new shape from the contours beneath?
And if it chose to lay itself down
in a new way, around a blind corner,
across hills you must climb without knowing
what's on the other side, who would not hanker
to be going, at all risks? Who wants to know
a story's end, or where a road will go?

❧ The Furthest Distances I've Travelled

Leontia Flynn 1974–

Like many folk, when first I saddled a rucksack,
feeling its weight on my back –
the way my spine
curved under it like a meridian –

I thought: Yes. This is how
to live. On the beaten track, the sherpa pass, between
   Krakow
and Zagreb, or the Siberian white
cells of scattered airports;

it came clear as over a tannoy
that in restlessness, in anony
mity:
was some kind of destiny.

So whether it was the scare stories about *Larium*
– the threats of delirium
and baldness – that lead me, not to a Western Union
wiring money with six words of Lithuanian,

but to this post office with a handful of bills
or a giro; and why, if I'm stuffing smalls
hastily into a holdall, I am less likely
to be catching a greyhound from Madison to Milwaukee

than to be doing some overdue laundry
is really beyond me.
However,
when, during routine evictions, I discover

alien pants, cinema stubs, the throwaway
comment – on a post–it – or a tiny stowaway
pressed flower amid bottom drawers,
I know these are my souvenirs

and, from these crushed valentines, this unravelled
sports sock, that the furthest distances I've travelled
have been those between people. And what survives
of holidaying briefly in their lives.

❧ Fuel

Naomi Shihab Nye 1952–

Even at this late date, sometimes I have to look up
the word "receive." I received his deep
and interested gaze.

A bean plant flourishes under the rain of sweet words.
Tell what you think—I'm listening.

The story ruffled its twenty leaves.

*

Once my teacher set me on a high stool
for laughing. She thought the eyes
of my classmates would whittle me to size.
But they said otherwise.

We'd laugh too if we knew how.

I pinned my gaze out the window
on a ripe line of sky.

That's where I was going.

❧ Escape

D.H. Lawrence 1885–1930

When we get out of the glass bottles of our own ego,
and when we escape like squirrels from turning in the
  cages of our personality
and get into the forest again,
we shall shiver with cold and fright
but things will happen to us
so that we don't know ourselves.

Cool, unlying life will rush in,
and passion will make our bodies taut with power,
we shall stamp our feet with new power
and old things will fall down,
we shall laugh, and institutions will curl up like burnt
  paper.

❧ Afternoon on a Hill

Edna St. Vincent Millay 1892–1950

I will be the gladdest thing
   Under the sun!
I will touch a hundred flowers
   And not pick one.

I will look at cliffs and clouds
   With quiet eyes,
Watch the wind bow down the grass,
   And the grass rise.

And when lights begin to show
   Up from the town,
I will mark which must be mine,
   And then start down!

❧ I Am Bound, I Am Bound, For A Distant Shore

Henry David Thoreau 1817–1862

I am bound, I am bound, for a distant shore,
By a lonely isle, by a far Azore,
There it is, there it is, the treasure I seek,
On the barren sands of a desolate creek

❧ The Lake Isle of Innisfree

W.B. Yeats 1865–1939

I will arise and go now, and go to Innisfree,
And a small cabin build there, of clay and wattles made;
Nine bean-rows will I have there, a hive for the
    honey-bee,
And live alone in the bee-loud glade.

And I shall have some peace there, for peace comes
    dropping slow,
Dropping from the veils of the morning to where the
    cricket sings;
There midnight's all a glimmer, and noon a purple glow,
And evening full of the linnet's wings.

I will arise and go now, for always night and day
I hear lake water lapping with low sounds by the shore;
While I stand on the roadway, or on the pavements grey,
I hear it in the deep heart's core.

❧ The River Village

Tu Fu 712–770

The river makes a bend and encircles the village with its
current.
All the long Summer, the affairs and occupations of the
river village are quiet and simple.
The swallows who nest in the beams go and come as they
please.
The gulls in the middle of the river enjoy one another,
they crowd together and touch one another.
My old wife paints a chess-board on paper.
My little sons hammer needles to make fish-hooks.
I have many illnesses, therefore my only necessities are
medicines.
Besides these, what more can so humble a man as I ask?

❧ The Old Pond

Matsuo Bashō 1644–1694
Translated by Robert Hass

The old pond—
a frog jumps in,
sound of water.

꩜ Half Asleep

Kobayashi Issa 1763–1828
Translated by Robert Hass

half asleep –
is that rainy season rain
again today?

❧ Let Us Go, Then, Exploring

Virginia Woolf 1882–1941

Let us go, then, exploring
This summer morning,
When all are adoring
The plum blossom and the bee.
And humming and hawing
Let us ask of the starling
What he may think
On the brink
Of the dustbin whence he picks
Among the sticks
Combings of scullion's hair.
What's life, we ask;
Life, Life, Life! cries the bird
As if he had heard.

❧ Song of the Open Road, 1

Walt Whitman 1819–1892

Afoot and light-hearted I take to the open road,
Healthy, free, the world before me,
The long brown path before me leading wherever I
   choose.

Henceforth I ask not good-fortune, I myself am good-
   fortune,
Henceforth I whimper no more, postpone no more, need
   nothing,
Done with indoor complaints, libraries, querulous
   criticisms,
Strong and content I travel the open road.

The earth, that is sufficient,
I do not want the constellations any nearer,
I know they are very well where they are,
I know they suffice for those who belong to them.

(Still here I carry my old delicious burdens,
I carry them, men and women, I carry them with me
   wherever I go,
I swear it is impossible for me to get rid of them,
I am fill'd with them, and I will fill them in return.)

❧ Recuerdo

Edna St. Vincent Millay 1892–1950

We were very tired, we were very merry—
We had gone back and forth all night on the ferry.
It was bare and bright, and smelled like a stable—
But we looked into a fire, we leaned across a table,
We lay on a hill-top underneath the moon;
And the whistles kept blowing, and the dawn came soon.

We were very tired, we were very merry—
We had gone back and forth all night on the ferry;
And you ate an apple, and I ate a pear,
From a dozen of each we had bought somewhere;
And the sky went wan, and the wind came cold,
And the sun rose dripping, a bucketful of gold.

We were very tired, we were very merry,
We had gone back and forth all night on the ferry.
We hailed, "Good morrow, mother!" to a shawl-covered
    head,
And bought a morning paper, which neither of us read;
And she wept, "God bless you!" for the apples and pears,
And we gave her all our money but our subway fares.

❧ Ah! Sun-flower

William Blake 1757–1827

Ah Sun-flower! weary of time,
Who countest the steps of the Sun:
Seeking after that sweet golden clime
Where the travellers journey is done.

Where the Youth pined away with desire,
And the pale Virgin shrouded in snow:
Arise from their graves and aspire,
Where my Sun-flower wishes to go.

🐚 Beachcomber

George Mackay Brown 1921–1996

Monday I found a boot –
Rust and salt leather.
I gave it back to the sea, to dance in.

Tuesday a spar of timber worth thirty bob.
Next winter
It will be a chair, a coffin, a bed.

Wednesday a half can of Swedish spirits.
I tilted my head.
The shore was cold with mermaids and angels.

Thursday I got nothing, seaweed,
A whale bone,
Wet feet and a loud cough.

Friday I held a seaman's skull,
Sand spilling from it
The way time is told on kirkyard stones.

Saturday a barrel of sodden oranges.
A Spanish ship
Was wrecked last month at The Kame.

Sunday, for fear of the elders,
I sit on my bum.
What's heaven? A sea chest with a thousand gold coins.

❧ To an Isle in the Water

W.B. Yeats 1865–1939

Shy one, shy one,
Shy one of my heart,
She moves in the firelight
Pensively apart.

She carries in the dishes,
And lays them in a row.
To an isle in the water
With her would I go.

She carries in the candles,
And lights the curtained room,
Shy in the doorway
And shy in the gloom;

And shy as a rabbit,
Helpful and shy.
To an isle in the water
With her would I fly.

❧ The Call

Charlotte Mew 1869–1928

From our low seat beside the fire
　　Where we have dozed and dreamed and watched the
　　　glow
　　Or raked the ashes, stopping so
We scarcely saw the sun or rain
　　Above, or looked much higher
Than this same quiet red or burned-out fire.
　　　　To-night we heard a call,
　　　　A rattle on the window-pane,
　　　　A voice on the sharp air,
And felt a breath stirring our hair,
　　A flame within us: Something swift and tall
　　Swept in and out and that was all.
Was it a bright or a dark angel? Who can know?
　　It left no mark upon the snow,
　　　　But suddenly it snapped the chain
　　　　Unbarred, flung wide the door
　　　　Which will not shut again;
And so we cannot sit here any more.

　　　　We must arise and go:
　　　　The world is cold without
　　　　And dark and hedged about
With mystery and enmity and doubt,
　　　　But we must go
　　　　Though yet we do not know
Who called, or what marks we shall leave upon the snow.

❧ The night is darkening round me

Emily Brontë 1818–1848

The night is darkening round me,
The wild winds coldly blow;
But a tyrant spell has bound me,
And I cannot, cannot go.

The giant trees are bending
Their bare boughs weighed with snow;
The storm is fast descending,
And yet I cannot go.

Clouds beyond clouds above me,
Wastes beyond wastes below;
But nothing drear can move me;
I will not, cannot go.

❧ XII

Sappho *c.* 630–570 BCE

In a dream I spoke with the Cyprus-born,
    And said to her,
"Mother of beauty, mother of joy,
Why hast thou given to men

"This thing called love, like the ache of a wound
    In beauty's side,
To burn and throb and be quelled for an hour
And never wholly depart?"

And the daughter of Cyprus said to me,
    "Child of the earth,
Behold, all things are born and attain,
But only as they desire,—

"The sun that is strong, the gods that are wise,
    The loving heart,
Deeds and knowledge and beauty and joy,—
But before all else was desire."

?❧ Jet

Tony Hoagland 1953–2018

Sometimes I wish I were still out
on the back porch, drinking jet fuel
with the boys, getting louder and louder
as the empty cans drop out of our paws
like booster rockets falling back to Earth

and we soar up into the summer stars.
Summer. The big sky river rushes overhead,
bearing asteroids and mist, blind fish
and old space suits with skeletons inside.
On Earth, men celebrate their hairiness,

and it is good, a way of letting life
out of the box, uncapping the bottle
to let the effervescence gush
through the narrow, usually constricted neck.

And now the crickets plug in their appliances
in unison, and then the fireflies flash
dots and dashes in the grass, like punctuation
for the labyrinthine, untrue tales of sex
someone is telling in the dark, though

no one really hears. We gaze into the night
as if remembering the bright unbroken planet
we once came from,
to which we will never
be permitted to return.
We are amazed how hurt we are.
We would give anything for what we have.

❧ Ode to a Nightingale

John Keats 1795–1821

My heart aches, and a drowsy numbness pains
  My sense, as though of hemlock I had drunk,
Or emptied some dull opiate to the drains
  One minute past, and Lethe-wards had sunk:
'Tis not through envy of thy happy lot,
  But being too happy in thine happiness,—
    That thou, light-winged Dryad of the trees
      In some melodious plot
Of beechen green, and shadows numberless,
  Singest of summer in full-throated ease.

O, for a draught of vintage! that hath been
  Cool'd a long age in the deep-delved earth,
Tasting of Flora and the country green,
  Dance, and Provençal song, and sunburnt mirth!
O for a beaker full of the warm South,
  Full of the true, the blushful Hippocrene,
    With beaded bubbles winking at the brim,
      And purple-stained mouth;
That I might drink, and leave the world unseen,
  And with thee fade away into the forest dim:

Fade far away, dissolve, and quite forget
  What thou among the leaves hast never known,
The weariness, the fever, and the fret
  Here, where men sit and hear each other groan;
Where palsy shakes a few, sad, last gray hairs,
  Where youth grows pale, and spectre-thin, and dies;
    Where but to think is to be full of sorrow
      And leaden-eyed despairs,
  Where Beauty cannot keep her lustrous eyes,
    Or new Love pine at them beyond to-morrow.

Away! away! for I will fly to thee,
  Not charioted by Bacchus and his pards,
But on the viewless wings of Poesy,
  Though the dull brain perplexes and retards:
Already with thee! tender is the night,
  And haply the Queen-Moon is on her throne,
    Cluster'd around by all her starry Fays;
      But here there is no light,
  Save what from heaven is with the breezes blown
    Through verdurous glooms and winding mossy ways.

I cannot see what flowers are at my feet,
  Nor what soft incense hangs upon the boughs,
But, in embalmed darkness, guess each sweet
  Wherewith the seasonable month endows
The grass, the thicket, and the fruit-tree wild;
  White hawthorn, and the pastoral eglantine;
    Fast fading violets cover'd up in leaves;
      And mid-May's eldest child,
  The coming musk-rose, full of dewy wine,
    The murmurous haunt of flies on summer eves.

Darkling I listen; and, for many a time
 I have been half in love with easeful Death,
Call'd him soft names in many a mused rhyme,
 To take into the air my quiet breath;
  Now more than ever seems it rich to die,
 To cease upon the midnight with no pain,
  While thou art pouring forth thy soul abroad
   In such an ecstasy!
 Still wouldst thou sing, and I have ears in vain—
  To thy high requiem become a sod.

Thou wast not born for death, immortal Bird!
 No hungry generations tread thee down;
The voice I hear this passing night was heard
 In ancient days by emperor and clown:
Perhaps the self-same song that found a path
 Through the sad heart of Ruth, when, sick for home,
  She stood in tears amid the alien corn;
   The same that oft-times hath
 Charm'd magic casements, opening on the foam
 Of perilous seas, in faery lands forlorn.

Forlorn! the very word is like a bell
 To toll me back from thee to my sole self!
Adieu! the fancy cannot cheat so well
 As she is fam'd to do, deceiving elf.
Adieu! adieu! thy plaintive anthem fades
 Past the near meadows, over the still stream,
  Up the hill-side; and now 'tis buried deep
   In the next valley-glades:
 Was it a vision, or a waking dream?
  Fled is that music:—Do I wake or sleep?

❧ High Flight

John Gillespie Magee Jr. 1922–1941

Oh! I have slipped the surly bonds of Earth
And danced the skies on laughter-silvered wings;
Sunward I've climbed, and joined the tumbling mirth
of sun-split clouds,—and done a hundred things
You have not dreamed of—wheeled and soared and swung
High in the sunlit silence. Hov'ring there,
I've chased the shouting wind along, and flung
My eager craft through footless halls of air ....

Up, up the long, delirious, burning blue
I've topped the wind-swept heights with easy grace
Where never lark nor ever eagle flew—
And, while with silent lifting mind I've trod
The high untrespassed sanctity of space,
Put out my hand, and touched the face of God.

❧ Dreams

Robert Herrick 1591–1674

Here we are all, by day; by night we're hurled
By dreams, each one, into a several world.

❧ Heaven-Haven

Gerard Manley Hopkins 1844–1889

A nun takes the veil

I have desired to go
  Where springs not fail,
To fields where flies no sharp and sided hail,
  And a few lilies blow.

And I have asked to be
  Where no storms come,
Where the green swell is in the havens dumb,
  And out of the swing of the sea.

❧ Eldorado

Edgar Allan Poe 1809–1849

Gaily bedight,
　A gallant knight,
In sunshine and in shadow,
　Had journeyed long,
　Singing a song,
In search of Eldorado.

　But he grew old—
　This knight so bold—
And o'er his heart a shadow—
　Fell as he found
　No spot of ground
That looked like Eldorado.

　And, as his strength
　Failed him at length,
He met a pilgrim shadow—
　'Shadow,' said he,
　'Where can it be—
This land of Eldorado?'

　'Over the Mountains
　Of the Moon,
Down the Valley of the Shadow,
　Ride, boldly ride,'
　The shade replied,—
'If you seek for Eldorado!'

🐦 The Song of Wandering Aengus

W.B. Yeats 1865–1939

I went out to the hazel wood,
Because a fire was in my head,
And cut and peeled a hazel wand,
And hooked a berry to a thread;
And when white moths were on the wing,
And moth-like stars were flickering out,
I dropped the berry in a stream
And caught a little silver trout.

When I had laid it on the floor
I went to blow the fire a-flame,
But something rustled on the floor,
And someone called me by my name:
It had become a glimmering girl
With apple blossom in her hair
Who called me by my name and ran
And faded through the brightening air.

Though I am old with wandering
Through hollow lands and hilly lands,
I will find out where she has gone,
And kiss her lips and take her hands;
And walk among long dappled grass,
And pluck till time and times are done,
The silver apples of the moon,
The golden apples of the sun.

❧ Skye Boat Song (Folk Song)

Anon

Speed, bonnie boat, like a bird on the wing
"Onward" the sailors cry!
Carry the lad that's born to be King
Over the sea to Skye.

Loud the winds cry, loud the waves roar,
Thunderclouds rend the air
Baffled our foes stand on the shore.
Follow they will not dare

Tho' the waves leap, soft shall ye sleep
Ocean's a royal bed
Rocked in the deep, Flora will keep
Watch by your weary head

Many's the lad fought on that day
Well the claymore could wield
When the night came, silently lay
Dead on Culloden's field

Burned are our homes, exile and death
Scatter the loyal men
Yet e'er the sword cool in the sheath
Charlie will come again

❧ Swing Low, Sweet Chariot

Wallace Willis 1814–1887

Swing low, sweet chariot,
Coming for to carry me home.
Swing low, sweet chariot,
Coming for to carry me home.

I looked over Jordan, and what did I see,
Coming for to carry me home?
A band of angels coming after me,
Coming for to carry me home.

Swing low, sweet chariot,
Coming for to carry me home.
Swing low, sweet chariot,
Coming for to carry me home.

If you get there before I do,
Coming for to carry me home.
Tell all my friends I'm coming too,
Coming for to carry me home.

Swing low, sweet chariot,
Coming for to carry me home.
Swing low, sweet chariot,
Coming for to carry me home.

The brightest day that ever I saw,
Coming for to carry me home,
When Jesus washed my sins away,
Coming for to carry me home.

Swing low, sweet chariot,
Coming for to carry me home.
Swing low, sweet chariot,
Coming for to carry me home.

I'm sometimes up and sometimes down,
Coming for to carry me home,
But still my soul feels heaven bound,
Coming for to carry me home.

Swing low, sweet chariot,
Coming for to carry me home.
Swing low, sweet chariot,
Coming for to carry me home.

❧ Escape at Bedtime

Robert Louis Stevenson 1850–1894

The lights from the parlour and kitchen shone out
Through the blinds and the windows and bars;
And high overhead and all moving about,
There were thousands of millions of stars.
There ne'er were such thousands of leaves on a tree,
Nor of people in church or the Park,
As the crowds of the stars that looked down upon me,
And that glittered and winked in the dark.

The Dog, and the Plough, and the Hunter, and all,
And the star of the sailor, and Mars,
These shone in the sky, and the pail by the wall
Would be half full of water and stars.
They saw me at last, and they chased me with cries,
And they soon had me packed into bed;
But the glory kept shining and bright in my eyes,
And the stars going round in my head.

❧ The Owl and the Pussy-Cat

Edward Lear 1812–1888

I

The Owl and the Pussy-cat went to sea
  In a beautiful pea-green boat,
They took some honey, and plenty of money,
  Wrapped up in a five-pound note.
The Owl looked up to the stars above,
  And sang to a small guitar,
"O lovely Pussy! O Pussy, my love,
  What a beautiful Pussy you are,
    You are,
    You are!
What a beautiful Pussy you are!"

II

Pussy said to the Owl, "You elegant fowl!
  How charmingly sweet you sing!
O let us be married! too long we have tarried:
  But what shall we do for a ring?"
They sailed away, for a year and a day,
  To the land where the Bong-Tree grows
And there in a wood a Piggy-wig stood
  With a ring at the end of his nose,
    His nose,
    His nose,
  With a ring at the end of his nose.

III

"Dear Pig, are you willing to sell for one shilling
  Your ring?" Said the Piggy, "I will."
So they took it away, and were married next day
  By the Turkey who lives on the hill.
They dined on mince, and slices of quince,
  Which they ate with a runcible spoon;
And hand in hand, on the edge of the sand,
  They danced by the light of the moon,
    The moon,
    The moon,
They danced by the light of the moon.

❧ Ulysses

Alfred, Lord Tennyson 1809–1892

It little profits that an idle king,
By this still hearth, among these barren crags,
Match'd with an aged wife, I mete and dole
Unequal laws unto a savage race,
That hoard, and sleep, and feed, and know not me.
I cannot rest from travel: I will drink
Life to the lees: All times I have enjoy'd
Greatly, have suffer'd greatly, both with those
That loved me, and alone, on shore, and when
Thro' scudding drifts the rainy Hyades
Vext the dim sea: I am become a name;
For always roaming with a hungry heart
Much have I seen and known; cities of men
And manners, climates, councils, governments,
Myself not least, but honour'd of them all;
And drunk delight of battle with my peers,
Far on the ringing plains of windy Troy.
I am a part of all that I have met;
Yet all experience is an arch wherethro'
Gleams that untravell'd world whose margin fades
For ever and forever when I move.
How dull it is to pause, to make an end,
To rust unburnish'd, not to shine in use!
As tho' to breathe were life! Life piled on life
Were all too little, and of one to me
Little remains: but every hour is saved
From that eternal silence, something more,
A bringer of new things; and vile it were
For some three suns to store and hoard myself,

And this gray spirit yearning in desire
To follow knowledge like a sinking star,
Beyond the utmost bound of human thought.

   This is my son, mine own Telemachus,
To whom I leave the sceptre and the isle,—
Well-loved of me, discerning to fulfil
This labour, by slow prudence to make mild
A rugged people, and thro' soft degrees
Subdue them to the useful and the good.
Most blameless is he, centred in the sphere
Of common duties, decent not to fail
In offices of tenderness, and pay
Meet adoration to my household gods,
When I am gone. He works his work, I mine.

   There lies the port; the vessel puffs her sail:
There gloom the dark, broad seas. My mariners,
Souls that have toil'd, and wrought, and thought with
    me—
That ever with a frolic welcome took
The thunder and the sunshine, and opposed
Free hearts, free foreheads—you and I are old;
Old age hath yet his honour and his toil;
Death closes all: but something ere the end,
Some work of noble note, may yet be done,
Not unbecoming men that strove with Gods.
The lights begin to twinkle from the rocks:
The long day wanes: the slow moon climbs: the deep
Moans round with many voices. Come, my friends,
'T is not too late to seek a newer world.
Push off, and sitting well in order smite
The sounding furrows; for my purpose holds
To sail beyond the sunset, and the baths

Of all the western stars, until I die.
It may be that the gulfs will wash us down:
It may be we shall touch the Happy Isles,
And see the great Achilles, whom we knew.
Tho' much is taken, much abides; and tho'
We are not now that strength which in old days
Moved earth and heaven, that which we are, we are;
One equal temper of heroic hearts,
Made weak by time and fate, but strong in will
To strive, to seek, to find, and not to yield.

August

Friends & Family

POETRY guides us through the maze that is life, in all of its stages. August marks the beginning of the end of summer, and is often spent with friends and family. With the start of the new academic or work year looming, it can be a transitional period, a time when our lives take great turns and we might bump into corners. But great poets can lead or at least sympathise with us, helping us reflect on our experiences and relationships, as well as to prepare for the future.

The month begins with a run of poetry on friendship, which culminates with an ode to the power of companionship between Man and Dog, before the punk poet John Cooper Clarke makes an appearance with 'I've Fallen in Love With My Wife', a tongue-in-cheek lyric on the joys of companionship in the later years of marriage: 'I'm her fella she's my mate/ She steals the chips right off my plate/ No wonder I'm losing weight/ I've fallen in love with my wife.'

Roger Robinson's deeply poignant ode 'Grace' then leads us on to the topic of parenthood. Robinson's poetry is often about finding unity through shared experience, and this ode to the 'Jamaican senior nurse/ who sang pop songs on her shift, like they were hymns' and looked after his premature son is no exception. And the confounding miracle of life might never have been better expressed than by Sylvia Plath's opening line, 'Love set you going like a fat gold watch.'

But what of how we feel about our parents? Billy Collins, one of the most popular poets in America, is a writer notably gifted at extracting the miraculous from the everyday. Here he gives perfect expression to the powerful allure of childhood memories, with a recollection of making his mother a lanyard that gives way to deeper reflections: 'not the worn truth/ that you can never repay your mother,/ but the rueful admission that when she took/ the two-tone lanyard from my hand,/ I was as sure as a boy could be/ that this useless, worthless thing I wove/ out of boredom would be enough to make us even.'

Longing for our missing parents is a theme which echoes throughout the month, and in these poems we see that even when it is not clear how poetry could guide us, it can offer catharsis or sympathy in our times of need. How else to explain the allure of Andrea Cohen's gut-punching poem 'The Committee Weighs In'? Or of Tony Harrison's lyric on both his deceased parents, which echoes Cohen's theme of the struggle to believe those who have always been there could ever be gone: 'I believe life ends with death, and that is all./ You haven't both gone shopping; just the same,/ in my new black leather phone book there's your name/ and the disconnected number I still call'?

Perhaps the wonder of poetry is its sympathy; no matter how hard to express or how complicated our personal problems may seem, the poets remind us that others have felt the same; that we are not alone. The poet and activist Warsan Shire's promise in 'Backwards', 'I can write the poem and make it disappear', carries the weight of all of literature's promises; that through the almost hallucinatory act of reading and imagining, for a moment we can escape from our pain.

The former Poet Laureate Carol Ann Duffy's heartbroken 'Empty Nest' begins a sequence of poems on more difficult relationship dynamics, especially those on the peripheries of the home. Both Duffy and Cecil Day-Lewis describe the 'pathos of a half-fledged thing set free' from its parents, concluding that 'love is proved in the letting go.' Of course, no collection on family troubles would be complete without Philip Larkin's poem 'This Be The Verse', with its iconic opening lines,

'They fuck you up, your mum and dad./ They may not mean to, but they do.' (Whether or not one ought to take the famously gloomy Larkin's wryly nihilistic advice – 'Get out as early as you can, / And don't have any kids yourself' – is a matter of personal choice!)

The works collected in this month highlight that difficult dynamics require difficult language, as we find in the almost monologic poetry of Chen Chen, Erica Gillingham and Toby Campion. Exploring themes of trauma and estrangement, using language that is raw, honest, and often deeply uncomfortable, these poets remind us that sometimes the only way to confront complex relationship issues is to express them.

Family and friendships, whether happy and harmonious or aching and entangled, can find their voice in a poem's gentle touch. If the poets are holding our hands and soothing us, or nourishing our minds through exposure to different perspectives, Roger Robinson's astute observation that 'poems are empathy machines' resonates profoundly here.

Dear child, the house pines
when you leave.
I research whether there is
any bird who grieves
over its empty nest.

Carol Ann Duffy

❧ Us Two

A.A. Milne 1882–1956

Wherever I am, there's always Pooh,
There's always Pooh and Me.
Whatever I do, he wants to do,
"Where are you going today?" says Pooh:
"Well, that's very odd 'cos I was too.
Let's go together," says Pooh, says he.
"Let's go together," says Pooh.

"What's twice eleven?" I said to Pooh.
("Twice what?" said Pooh to Me.)
"I think it ought to be twenty-two."
"Just what I think myself," said Pooh.
"It wasn't an easy sum to do,
But that's what it is," said Pooh, said he.
"That's what it is," said Pooh.

"Let's look for dragons," I said to Pooh.
"Yes, let's," said Pooh to Me.
We crossed the river and found a few –
"Yes, those are dragons all right," said Pooh.
"As soon as I saw their beaks I knew.
That's what they are," said Pooh, said he.
"That's what they are," said Pooh.

"Let's frighten the dragons," I said to Pooh.
"That's right," said Pooh to Me.
"I'm not afraid," I said to Pooh,
And I held his paw and I shouted "Shoo!
Silly old dragons!" – and off they flew.
"I wasn't afraid," said Pooh, said he,
"I'm never afraid with you."

So wherever I am, there's always Pooh,
There's always Pooh and Me.
"What would I do?" I said to Pooh,
"If it wasn't for you," and Pooh said: "True,
It isn't much fun for One, but Two,
Can stick together," says Pooh, says he. "That's how
    it is," says Pooh.

❧ Love and Friendship

Emily Brontë 1818–1848

Love is like the wild rose-briar,
Friendship like the holly-tree—
The holly is dark when the rose-briar blooms
But which will bloom most constantly?

The wild rose-briar is sweet in spring,
Its summer blossoms scent the air;
Yet wait till winter comes again
And who will call the wild-briar fair?

Then scorn the silly rose-wreath now
And deck thee with the holly's sheen,
That when December blights thy brow
He still may leave thy garland green.

❧ You Smile Upon Your Friend To-day

A.E. Housman 1859–1936

You smile upon your friend to-day,
To-day his ills are over;
You hearken to the lover's say,
And happy is the lover.

'Tis late to hearken, late to smile,
But better late than never:
I shall have lived a little while
Before I die for ever.

❧ Sunshine After Cloud

Josephine D. Heard 1861–1924

Come, "Will," let's be good friends again,
  Our wrongs let's be forgetting,
For words bring only useless pain,
  So wherefore then be fretting.

Let's lay aside imagined wrongs,
  And ne'er give way to grieving,
Life should be filled with joyous songs,
  No time left for deceiving.

I'll try and not give way to wrath,
  Nor be so often crying;
There must some thorns be in our path,
  Let's move them now by trying.

How, like a foolish pair were we,
  To fume about a letter;
Time is so precious, you and me;
  Must spend ours doing better.

❧ The Arrow and the Song

Henry Wadsworth Longfellow 1807–1882

I shot an arrow into the air,
It fell to earth, I knew not where;
For, so swiftly it flew, the sight
Could not follow it in its flight.

I breathed a song into the air,
It fell to earth, I knew not where;
For who has sight so keen and strong,
That it can follow the flight of song?

Long, long afterward, in an oak
I found the arrow, still unbroke;
And the song, from beginning to end,
I found again in the heart of a friend.

ॐ And That

Raymond Antrobus 1986–

After seeing a childhood friend outside a chicken shop in
Dalston

"Chicken wings / and that
Boss man / salt in them / and that

Don't assault man / give man a nap-
Kin / Big man / no steroid / and that

Dark times / new street lights / and that
How's man? / I'm getting by / and that

Still / boy dem / harass
Not beefin' / not tagged / man / still trapped

Cycle man / I peddle / and that
On road / new pavements / leveled / and that

Crackney changed / still / stay dwelling / and that
Paradise moves / but I got to land grab

We E8 / East man / ain't got to adapt
Our Kingdom / got no land to hand back

Man / chat breeze / chat
Trade winds / and that

You out ends / got good job / legit / and that?
Locked off man dem / stay plotting / and that

Rah, Ray / flower shorts? / You hipster / in that
Man gone / Vegan? / no chicken wings / and that"

❧ The Power of the Dog

Rudyard Kipling 1865–1936

There is sorrow enough in the natural way
From men and women to fill our day;
And when we are certain of sorrow in store,
Why do we always arrange for more?
Brothers and Sisters, I bid you beware
Of giving your heart to a dog to tear.

Buy a pup and your money will buy
Love unflinching that cannot lie—
Perfect passion and worship fed
By a kick in the ribs or a pat on the head.
Nevertheless it is hardly fair
To risk your heart for a dog to tear.

When the fourteen years which Nature permits
Are closing in asthma, or tumour, or fits,
And the vet's unspoken prescription runs
To lethal chambers or loaded guns,
Then you will find—it's your own affair—
But . . . you've given your heart to a dog to tear.

When the body that lived at your single will,
With its whimper of welcome, is stilled (how still!).
When the spirit that answered your every mood
Is gone—wherever it goes—for good,
You will discover how much you care,
And will give your heart to a dog to tear.

We've sorrow enough in the natural way,
When it comes to burying Christian clay.
Our loves are not given, but only lent,
At compound interest of cent per cent.
Though it is not always the case, I believe,
That the longer we've kept 'em, the more do we grieve:
For, when debts are payable, right or wrong,
A short-time loan is as bad as a long—
So why in—Heaven (before we are there)
Should we give our hearts to a dog to tear?

❧ I've Fallen in Love With My Wife

John Cooper Clarke 1949–

The doorbell used to say ding dong
But now it breaks out into song
If I'm forlorn it ain't for long
Could I be wrong or have I
Fallen in love with my wife

Fare thee well my fairy fey
We cared so slightly anyway
Call me Krazy with a Kapital K
I've fallen in love with my wife

I've fallen in love with my wife
She populates my days
With marital breakdown running rife
I have to keep her under my gaze

You love somebody – set them free
That don't make no sense to me
I'm keeping her under lock and key
I've fallen in love with my wife

Rainbows and butterflies
Occupy the summer skies
Imagine my surprise
I've fallen in love with my wife

I've fallen in love with my wife
She populates my days
It's keeping me awake at night
My head stuck in this funky smaze

Every time I talk I mumble
Every time I walk I stumble
I'm dancing like a drunken uncle
I've fallen in love with my wife

I've fallen in love with my wife
She populates my days
She's not that far from a carving knife
I have to keep her in my gaze

I don't swear but what the hey
I'm all right and she's OK
Get out of our fucking way
I've fallen in love with my wife

I'm her fella she's my mate
She steals the chips right off my plate
No wonder I'm losing weight
I've fallen in love with my wife

I steal a kiss she takes the piss
We lived a life of ignorant bliss
All that and now this
I've fallen in love with my wife

 Grace

Roger Robinson 1970–

That year we danced to green bleeps on screen.
My son had come early, just the 1kg of him,
all big head, bulging eyes and blue veins.

On the ward I met Grace. A Jamaican senior nurse
who sang pop songs on her shift, like they were hymns.
"Your son feisty. Y'see him just ah pull off the breathing
    mask."

People spoke of her in half tones down these carbolic halls.
Even the doctors gave way to her, when it comes
    to putting a line into my son's nylon thread of a vein.

She'd warn junior doctors with trembling hands: "Me only
    letting you try twice."
On her night shift she pulls my son's incubator into her
    room,
no matter the tangled confusion of wires and machine.

When the consultant told my wife and I on morning
    rounds
that he's not sure my son will live, and if he lives he might
    never leave the hospital,
she pulled us quickly aside: "Him have no right to say
    that—just raw so."

Another consultant tells the nurses to stop feeding a baby,
   who will soon die,
and she commands her loyal nurses to feed him. "No baby
   must dead
wid a hungry belly." And she'd sit in the dark, rocking
   that well-fed baby,

held to her bosom, slowly humming the melody of
   "Happy" by Pharrell.
And I think, if by some chance, I'm not here and my son's
   life should flicker,
then Grace, she should be the one.

ᙦ Morning Song

Sylvia Plath 1932–1963

Love set you going like a fat gold watch.
The midwife slapped your footsoles, and your bald cry
Took its place among the elements.

Our voices echo, magnifying your arrival. New statue.
In a drafty museum, your nakedness
Shadows our safety. We stand round blankly as walls.

I'm no more your mother
Than the cloud that distills a mirror to reflect its own slow
Effacement at the wind's hand.

All night your moth-breath
Flickers among the flat pink roses. I wake to listen:
A far sea moves in my ear.

One cry, and I stumble from bed, cow-heavy and floral
In my Victorian nightgown.
Your mouth opens clean as a cat's. The window square

Whitens and swallows its dull stars. And now you try
Your handful of notes;
The clear vowels rise like balloons.

⁊❧ Infant Joy

William Blake 1757–1827

I have no name
I am but two days old.—
What shall I call thee?
I happy am
Joy is my name,—
Sweet joy befall thee!

Pretty joy!
Sweet joy but two days old,
Sweet joy I call thee;
Thou dost smile.
I sing the while
Sweet joy befall thee.

❧ Happy Birthday Moon

Raymond Antrobus 1986–

Dad reads aloud. I follow his finger across the page.
Sometimes his finger moves past words, tracing white
  space.
He makes the Moon say something new every night
to his deaf son who slurs his speech.

Sometimes his finger moves past words, tracing white
  space.
Tonight he gives the Moon my name, but I can't say it,
his deaf son who slurs his speech.
Dad taps the page, says, *try again*.

Tonight he gives the Moon my name, but I can't say it.
I say *Rain-nan Akabok*. He laughs.
Dad taps the page, says, *try again*,
but I like making him laugh. I say my mistake again.

I say *Rain-nan Akabok*. He laughs,
says, *Raymond you're something else*.
I like making him laugh. I say my mistake again.
Rain-nan Akabok. What else will help us?

He says, *Raymond you're something else*.
I'd like to be the Moon, the bear, even the rain.
Rain-nan Akabok, what else will help us
hear each other, really hear each other?

I'd like to be the Moon, the bear, even the rain.
Dad makes the Moon say something new every night
and we hear each other, really hear each other.
As Dad reads aloud, I follow his finger across the page.

❧ On Children

Kahlil Gibran 1883–1931

And a woman who held a babe against her bosom said,
   Speak to us of Children.
   And he said:
Your children are not your children.
They are the sons and daughters of Life's longing for
   itself.
They come through you but not from you,
And though they are with you yet they belong not to you.

You may give them your love but not your thoughts,
For they have their own thoughts.
You may house their bodies but not their souls,
For their souls dwell in the house of tomorrow, which you
   cannot visit, not even in your dreams.
You may strive to be like them, but seek not to make them
   like you.
For life goes not backward nor tarries with yesterday.
You are the bows from which your children as living
   arrows are sent forth.
The archer sees the mark upon the path of the infinite, and
   He bends you with His might that His arrows may go
   swift and far.
Let your bending in the archer's hand be for gladness;
For even as He loves the arrow that flies, so He loves also
   the bow that is stable.

❧ The Lanyard

Billy Collins 1941–

The other day I was ricocheting slowly
off the blue walls of this room,
moving as if underwater from typewriter to piano,
from bookshelf to an envelope lying on the floor,
when I found myself in the L section of the dictionary
where my eyes fell upon the word lanyard.

No cookie nibbled by a French novelist
could send one into the past more suddenly—
a past where I sat at a workbench at a camp
by a deep Adirondack lake
learning how to braid long thin plastic strips
into a lanyard, a gift for my mother.

I had never seen anyone use a lanyard
or wear one, if that's what you did with them,
but that did not keep me from crossing
strand over strand again and again
until I had made a boxy
red and white lanyard for my mother.

She gave me life and milk from her breasts,
and I gave her a lanyard.
She nursed me in many a sick room,
lifted spoons of medicine to my lips,
laid cold face-cloths on my forehead,
and then led me out into the airy light

and taught me to walk and swim,
and I, in turn, presented her with a lanyard.
Here are thousands of meals, she said,
and here is clothing and a good education.
And here is your lanyard, I replied,
which I made with a little help from a counselor.

Here is a breathing body and a beating heart,
strong legs, bones and teeth,
and two clear eyes to read the world, she whispered,
and here, I said, is the lanyard I made at camp.
And here, I wish to say to her now,
is a smaller gift—not the worn truth

that you can never repay your mother,
but the rueful admission that when she took
the two-tone lanyard from my hand,
I was as sure as a boy could be
that this useless, worthless thing I wove
out of boredom would be enough to make us even.

🐦 An Interesting Fact About One of My Relatives

Ian McMillan 1956–

My

great great great great
great great great great
great great great great
great great great great
great great great great
great great great great
great great great great

grandad is very old.

❧ Invisible Kisses

Lemn Sissay 1967–

If there was ever one
Whom when you were sleeping
Would wipe your tears
When in dreams you were weeping;
Who would offer you time
When others demand;
Whose love lay more infinite
Than grains of sand.

If there was ever one
To whom you could cry;
Who would gather each tear
And blow it dry;
Who would offer help
On the mountains of time;
Who would stop to let each sunset
Soothe the jaded mind.

If there was ever one
To whom when you run
Will push back the clouds
So you are bathed in sun;
Who would open arms
If you would fall;
Who would show you everything
If you lost it all.

If there was ever one
Who when you achieve
Was there before the dream
And even then believed;
Who would clear the air
When it's full of loss;
Who would count love
Before the cost.

If there was ever one
Who when you are cold
Will summon warm air
For your hands to hold;
Who would make peace
In pouring pain,
Make laughter fall
In falling rain.

If there was ever one
Who can offer you this and more;
Who in keyless rooms
Can open doors;
Who in open doors
Can see open fields
And in open fields
See harvests yield.

Then see only my face
In reflection of these tides
Through the clear water
Beyond the river side.
All I can send is love
In all that this is
A poem and a necklace
Of invisible kisses.

❧ Empty Nest

Carol Ann Duffy 1955–

Dear child, the house pines when you leave.
I research whether there is any bird who grieves
over its empty nest.

                               Your vacant room
is a still-life framed by the unclosed door;
read by sunlight, an open book on the floor.

I fold the laundry; hang your flower dress
in darkness. Forget-me-nots.

          *

Beyond the tall fence, I hear horse-chestnuts
counting themselves.

                      Then autumn; Christmas.
You come and go, singing. Then ice; snowdrops.

Our home hides its face in hands of silence.

I knew mothering, but not this other thing
which hefts my heart each day. Heavier.
Now I know.

          *

This is the shy sorrow. It will not speak up.
I play one chord on the piano;

                      it vanishes, tactful,
as dusk muffles the garden; a magpie staring from its
    branch.
The marble girl standing by the bench.

From the local church, bells like a spelling.
And the evening star like a text.
And then what next . . .

❧ Walking Away

Cecil Day-Lewis 1904–1972

It is eighteen years ago, almost to the day –
A sunny day with leaves just turning,
The touch-lines new-ruled – since I watched you play
Your first game of football, then, like a satellite
Wrenched from its orbit, go drifting away

Behind a scatter of boys. I can see
You walking away from me towards the school
With the pathos of a half-fledged thing set free
Into a wilderness, the gait of one
Who finds no path where the path should be.

That hesitant figure, eddying away
Like a winged seed loosened from its parent stem,
Has something I never quite grasp to convey
About nature's give-and-take – the small, the scorching
Ordeals which fire one's irresolute clay.

I have had worse partings, but none that so
Gnaws at my mind still. Perhaps it is roughly
Saying what God alone could perfectly show –
How selfhood begins with a walking away,
And love is proved in the letting go.

❧ I See You Dancing, Father

Brendan Kennelly 1936–2021

No sooner downstairs after the night's rest
And in the door
Than you started to dance a step
In the middle of the kitchen floor.

And as you danced
You whistled.
You made your own music
Always in tune with yourself.

Well, nearly always, anyway.
You're buried now
In Lislaughtin Abbey
And whenever I think of you

I go back beyond the old man
Mind and body broken
To find the unbroken man.
It is the moment before the dance begins,

Your lips are enjoying themselves
Whistling an air.
Whatever happens or cannot happen
In the time I have to spare
I see you dancing, father.

?» This Be The Verse

Philip Larkin 1922–1985

They fuck you up, your mum and dad.
　They may not mean to, but they do.
They fill you with the faults they had
　And add some extra, just for you.

But they were fucked up in their turn
　By fools in old-style hats and coats,
Who half the time were soppy-stern
　And half at one another's throats.

Man hands on misery to man.
　It deepens like a coastal shelf.
Get out as early as you can,
　And don't have any kids yourself.

❧ Let's Make a Baby with Science

Erica Gillingham 1984–

We can't fuck our way to a family
so let's do the furthest thing possible
from the intimacy of our bedroom.

Let's invite a dozen medical professionals
to ask us invasive questions with varying
degrees of empathy & bedside manner.

Let's test my veins, my blood, my uterus,
my textbook ovaries until we lose track
of our week-on-week appointments.

Let's find ourselves speechless after each shot,
not knowing how to respond to each other,
syringes empty, sharp's box lying at our feet.

Let's turn down invitations to all-night discos,
weekend benders, & sweaty basement raves
because we've got at-home stimulants to do.

Let's call the process a cycle, as if it's natural,
then spend two weeks worrying about having
enough piss in my bladder for the pregnancy test.

And when it doesn't work, think it should work,
we won't know why, may never know why,
then we'll do it all over again.

And again.

And again.

And again.

❧ Advice

Dan Gerber 1940–

You know how, after it rains,
my father told me one August afternoon
when I struggled with something
hurtful my best friend had said,
how worms come out and
crawl all over the sidewalk
and it stays a big mess
a long time after it's over
if you step on them?

Leave them alone,
he went on to say,
after clearing his throat,
and when the rain stops,
they crawl back into the ground.

৯ I Invite My Parents to a Dinner Party

Chen Chen 1989–

In the invitation, I tell them for the seventeenth time
(the fourth in writing), that I am gay.

In the invitation, I include a picture of my boyfriend
& write, *You've met him two times. But this time,*

*you will ask him things other than can you pass the
whatever. You will ask him*

*about him. You will enjoy dinner. You will be
enjoyable. Please RSVP.*

They RSVP. They come.
They sit at the table & ask my boyfriend

the first of the conversation starters I slip them
upon arrival: *How is work going?*

I'm like the kid in *Home Alone*, orchestrating
every movement of a proper family, as if a pair

of scary yet deeply incompetent burglars
is watching from the outside.

My boyfriend responds in his chipper way.
I pass my father a bowl of fish ball soup—*So comforting,*

isn't it? My mother smiles her best
Sitting with Her Son's Boyfriend

Who Is a Boy Smile. I smile my Hurray for Doing
a Little Better Smile.

Everyone eats soup.
Then, my mother turns

to me, whispers in Mandarin, *Is he coming with you*
for Thanksgiving? My good friend is & she wouldn't like

this. I'm like the kid in *Home Alone,* pulling
on the string that makes my cardboard mother

more motherly, except she is
not cardboard, she is

already, exceedingly my mother. Waiting
for my answer.

While my father opens up
a *Boston Globe,* when the invitation

clearly stated: *No security*
blankets. I'm like the kid

in *Home Alone,* except the home
is my apartment, & I'm much older, & not alone,

& not the one who needs
to learn, has to—*Remind me*

what's in that recipe again, my boyfriend says
to my mother, as though they have always, easily

talked. As though no one has told him
many times, what a nonlinear slapstick meets

slasher flick meets psychological
pit he is now co-starring in.

Remind me, he says
to our family.

?> The Committee Weighs In

Andrea Cohen 1961–

I tell my mother
I've won the Nobel Prize.

Again? she says. Which
discipline this time?

It's a little game
we play: I pretend

I'm somebody, she
pretends she isn't dead.

❧ George Square

Jackie Kay 1961–

My seventy-seven-year-old father
put his reading glasses on
to help my mother do the buttons
on the back of her dress.
'What a pair the two of us are!'
my mother said, 'Me with my sore wrist,
you with your bad eyes, your soft thumbs!'
And off they went, my two parents
to march against the war in Iraq,
him with his plastic hips, her with her arthritis,
to congregate at George Square, where the banners
waved at each other like old friends, flapping,
where they'd met for so many marches over their years,
for peace on earth, for pity's sake, for peace, for peace.

❧ When the Stranger Called me a Faggot

Toby Campion 1993–

I did not blink

instead   this time   my mouth filled with
Grimsby's chip cone, wooden forks
and Aylestone Leisure Centre, rolling hills, walks to
    school,
my first cigarette bought off Josh Baker for 50p
and the taste of being short-changed and the taste of being
    told
it is fair, K-Swiss, The Old Horse, my overworked father,
uncles asking about girlfriends at Christmas, my cousin's
    knee,
my broken nose and the kitchen roll unable to soak up
a family's damage, funeral faces, graffiti
on the back of our livers and Churchgate, Maryland
    Chicken,
free entry before eleven, bottles tossed into dancing
    crowds,
lips greeting glass with crimson splutterings of *hallelujah*,
and fifth period French, savages born of boredom,
fighting Ashley down the science block, crowd of camera-
    phones
blocking us in, no way out for one
and Nickesh and Chris and Sam,
Mecca Bingo and wash brook, the boy who got snatched,
chewing gum sticking eyelashes together,
football practice and get it together lads,

my hand on his leg, shower room and eyes forward lads,
his hand in my mouth
and or what or what or what.

and my new friends said,
we haven't heard you like that before

and I said,
you haven't heard me.

੨ Backwards

Warsan Shire 1988–

The poem can start with him walking backwards into a
    room.
He takes off his jacket and sits down for the rest of his life;
that's how we bring Dad back.
I can make the blood run back up my nose, ants rushing
    into a hole.
We grow into smaller bodies, my breasts disappear,
your cheeks soften, teeth sink back into gums.
I can make us loved, just say the word.
Give them stumps for hands if even once they touched us
    without consent,
I can write the poem and make it disappear.
Step-Dad spits liquor back into glass,
Mum's body rolls back up the stairs, the bone pops back
    into place,
maybe she keeps the baby.
Maybe we're okay kid?
I'll rewrite this whole life and this time there'll be so much
    love,
you won't be able to see beyond it.

You won't be able to see beyond it,
I'll rewrite this whole life and this time there'll be so much
   love.
Maybe we're okay kid,
maybe she keeps the baby.
Mum's body rolls back up the stairs, the bone pops back
   into place,
Step-Dad spits liquor back into glass.
I can write the poem and make it disappear,
give them stumps for hands if even once they touched us
   without consent,
I can make us loved, just say the word.
Your cheeks soften, teeth sink back into gums
we grow into smaller bodies, my breasts disappear.
I can make the blood run back up my nose, ants rushing
   into a hole,
that's how we bring Dad back.
He takes off his jacket and sits down for the rest of his life.
The poem can start with him walking backwards into a
   room.

❧ Long Distance II

Tony Harrison 1937–

Though my mother was already two years dead
Dad kept her slippers warming by the gas,
put hot water bottles her side of the bed
and still went to renew her transport pass.

You couldn't just drop in. You had to phone.
He'd put you off an hour to give him time
to clear away her things and look alone
as though his still raw love were such a crime.

He couldn't risk my blight of disbelief
though sure that very soon he'd hear her key
scrape in the rusted lock and end his grief.
He knew she'd just popped out to get the tea.

I believe life ends with death, and that is all.
You haven't both gone shopping; just the same,
in my new black leather phone book there's your name
and the disconnected number I still call.

❧ Look there he goes even now, my father

Daljit Nagra 1966–

Look there he goes even now, my father,
into some other world, all my life
I have been harbour-struck
trying to make him appear
from wherever he went
the years before
I was born . . .

❧ August Day

Jane Hirshfield 1953–

You work with what you are given—
today I am blessed, today I am given luck.

It takes the shape of a dozen ripening fruit trees,
a curtain of pole beans, a thicket of berries.
It takes the shape of a dozen empty hours.

In them is neither love nor love's muster of losses,
in them is no chance for harm or for good.
Does even my humanness matter?
A bear would be equally happy, this August day,
fat on the simple sweetness plucked between thorns.

There are some who may think, "How pitiful, how
    lonely."
Others must murmer, "How lazy."

I agree with them all: pitiful, lonely, lazy.
Lost to the earth and to heaven,
thoroughly drunk on its whiskeys, I wander my kingdom.

❧ Blackberry-picking

Seamus Heaney 1939–2013

for Philip Hobsbaum

Late August, given heavy rain and sun
For a full week, the blackberries would ripen.
At first, just one, a glossy purple clot
Among others, red, green, hard as a knot.
You ate that first one and its flesh was sweet
Like thickened wine: summer's blood was in it
Leaving stains upon the tongue and lust for
Picking. Then red ones inked up and that hunger
Sent us out with milk cans, pea tins, jam-pots
Where briars scratched and wet grass bleached our boots.
Round hayfields, cornfields and potato-drills
We trekked and picked until the cans were full,
Until the tinkling bottom had been covered
With green ones, and on top big dark blobs burned
Like a plate of eyes. Our hands were peppered
With thorn pricks, our palms sticky as Bluebeard's.

We hoarded the fresh berries in the byre.
But when the bath was filled we found a fur,
A rat-grey fungus, glutting on our cache.
The juice was stinking too. Once off the bush
The fruit fermented, the sweet flesh would turn sour.
I always felt like crying. It wasn't fair
That all the lovely canfuls smelt of rot.
Each year I hoped they'd keep, knew they would not.

September

Inspiration

T HE start of the academic year – September is a month in which to be inspired. Descended from the Latin *'inspirare'* (to blow or breathe into), the figurative sense of 'inspiration' arrived via the Christian sense of 'breathing spirit into something'. The greatest poets are great philosophers, and, especially in a secular age, their words are a powerful conduit to the wisdom of our ancestors.

W.B. Yeats once said that there are two types of poet; those who rouse, and those who console. The poems collected here fall into both categories, with works ranging from Dylan Thomas's stirring villanelle, 'Do not go gentle into that good night' to the delicate verse of Danez Smith and Tony Hoagland, reminding us to find the time 'to sit out in the sun and listen'. The poems collected for this month let us break bread with the brilliant dead and offer advice from our contemporary poets, with sage and rousing words on a broad variety of themes. Percy Bysshe Shelley's 'Ozymandias' counsels us to avoid excessive pride in positions of power. Ron Padgett and Jenny Joseph encourage us to embrace old age, although in completely different ways, and Audre Lorde appears twice with profound and rallying words on issues of sex and race.

It is often striking how these poems take on lives of their own when they inspire their readers. William Wordsworth's father encouraged him to learn poems by heart, calling the mental library of poetry his 'golden store', which would keep him company throughout his life. He recognised that a poem can stay with you and be drawn upon in times of need. There is perhaps no greater example of this than William Ernest Henley's rousing poem 'Invictus', meaning 'unconquered' in Latin. Henley himself had a difficult life and lost a leg to tuberculosis at the age of twelve; the poem provided the name Invictus Games for the sporting event Prince Harry founded for injured soldiers. During South Africa's period of Apartheid, Nelson Mandela drew on his memory of Henley's poem during the twenty-seven years he spent incarcerated on Robben Island. Its powerful last lines, 'I am the master of my fate,/ I am the captain of my soul' have inspired both heroes like Mandela and countless private individuals, offering strength in dark times.

In endlessly varied circumstances, these poems offer universal truths. Reading the works of poets from across the ages shows us how much has changed and how much has stayed the same. A recurrent message is to let nature be your teacher; whether Victor Hugo's advice to 'Be like the bird' or Alfred, Lord Tennyson's advice to live like 'yon oak', poets harvest lessons from nature. And from Robert Frost's gently nudging couplets in 'Nothing Gold Can Stay' to D.H. Lawrence's stern reminder that 'A small bird will drop frozen dead from a bough / without ever having felt sorry for itself', poets have a store of tones and techniques with which they try to divert our thoughts. Another recurring theme is advice simply to be kind; from Philip Larkin's sombre account of accidentally killing a hedgehog to Adam Lindsay Gordon's pithy summary that 'Life is mostly froth and bubble' – poets offer much for us to muse over.

Yet as much as a piece of poetic wisdom might seem universal, behind some poems is an inspiring personal history. After his father's death, the lyric poet W.H. Davies used his inheritance to travel from Wales across the Atlantic; as he roamed the US and Canada as a homeless drifter, he sustained himself by begging. In 'Leisure', Davies' bucolic reminder to slow down, pause and be mindful is enriched by the context of his incredible commitment to rejection of a conventionally busy life.

The final poem in the month is by Langston Hughes, one of the first poets to fuse the offbeat, irregular rhythms of jazz with poetry. His unpretentious 'Advice', with its upbeat musicality, reminds us that the gift of poetry is to inspire not only with its sense but its sound.

What is this life if, full of care,
We have no time to stand and stare?

W.H. Davies

❧ The Mower

Philip Larkin 1922–1985

The mower stalled, twice; kneeling, I found
A hedgehog jammed up against the blades,
Killed. It had been in the long grass.

I had seen it before, and even fed it, once.
Now I had mauled its unobtrusive world
Unmendably. Burial was no help:

Next morning I got up and it did not.
The first day after a death, the new absence
Is always the same; we should be careful

Of each other, we should be kind
While there is still time.

❧ Love Listen

Ann Gray 1946–

Let's love, listen, take time
when time is all we have.
Let's be unafraid to be kind,
learn to disregard the bad
if the good outweighs it daily.
Let's make a gift of silence,
the day's hushing into dark,
and when we hold each other
let's always be astonished
we are where we want to be.
Let's hope to age together,
but if we can't, let's promise now
to remember how we shone
when we were at our best,
when we were most ourselves.

❧ A Litany for Survival

Audre Lorde 1934–1992

For those of us who live at the shoreline
standing upon the constant edges of decision
crucial and alone
for those of us who cannot indulge
the passing dreams of choice
who love in doorways coming and going
in the hours between dawns
looking inward and outward
at once before and after
seeking a now that can breed
futures
like bread in our children's mouths
so their dreams will not reflect
the death of ours;

For those of us
who were imprinted with fear
like a faint line in the center of our foreheads
learning to be afraid with our mother's milk
for by this weapon
this illusion of some safety to be found
the heavy-footed hoped to silence us
For all of us
this instant and this triumph
We were never meant to survive.

And when the sun rises we are afraid
it might not remain
when the sun sets we are afraid
it might not rise in the morning
when our stomachs are full we are afraid
of indigestion
when our stomachs are empty we are afraid
we may never eat again
when we are loved we are afraid
love will vanish
when we are alone we are afraid
love will never return
and when we speak we are afraid
our words will not be heard
nor welcomed
but when we are silent
we are still afraid

So it is better to speak
remembering
we were never meant to survive.

❧ Courage is a Muscle

Salena Godden 1969–

Courage is the muscle
we use when we speak,
if we're being talked over
and told we're too weak.
And when we get weary
and when it gets tough,
it's our united courage says –
Enough is enough.

Courage is the muscle
we work night and day,
to get equal rights
to get equal pay.
Our blood is taxed
our blood is shame,
our courage unites us
for we all bleed the same.

Courage is the muscle
we flex when we must,
courage is the muscle
for truth and for trust.
Courage is the muscle
we use when we speak,
if we're being walked over
and told we're too weak.

And when we get weary
we march side by side,
1000 years we're still marching
with courage and with pride.

⅋ Warning

Jenny Joseph 1932–2018

When I am an old woman I shall wear purple
With a red hat which doesn't go, and doesn't suit me.
And I shall spend my pension on brandy and summer
    gloves
And satin sandals, and say we've no money for butter.
I shall sit down on the pavement when I'm tired
And gobble up samples in shops and press alarm bells
And run my stick along the public railings
And make up for the sobriety of my youth.
I shall go out in my slippers in the rain
And pick flowers in other people's gardens
And learn to spit.

You can wear terrible shirts and grow more fat
And eat three pounds of sausages at a go
Or only bread and pickle for a week
And hoard pens and pencils and beermats and things in
    boxes.

But now we must have clothes that keep us dry
And pay our rent and not swear in the street
And set a good example for the children.
We must have friends to dinner and read the papers.

But maybe I ought to practise a little now?
So people who know me are not too shocked and surprised
When suddenly I am old, and start to wear purple.

❧ I Forgive You, Maria

Stevie Smith 1902–1971

I forgive you Maria
Things can never be the same,
But I forgive you Maria
Though I think you were to blame,
I forgive you Maria,
I can never forget,
But I forgive you, Maria
Kindly remember that.

❧ Patience

Edith Wharton 1862–1937

Patience and I have traveled hand in hand
So many days that I have grown to trace
The lines of sad, sweet beauty in her face,
And all its veilèd depths to understand.

Not beautiful is she to eyes profane;
Silent and unrevealed her holy charms;
But, like a mother's, her serene, strong arms
Uphold my footsteps on the path of pain.

I long to cry,—her soft voice whispers, "Nay!"
I seek to fly, but she restrains my feet;
In wisdom stern, yet in compassion sweet,
She guides my helpless wanderings, day by day.

O my Beloved, life's golden visions fade,
And one by one life's phantom joys depart;
They leave a sudden darkness in the heart,
And patience fills their empty place instead.

❧ Who Said It Was Simple

Audre Lorde 1934–1992

There are so many roots to the tree of anger
that sometimes the branches shatter
before they bear.

Sitting in Nedicks
the women rally before they march
discussing the problematic girls
they hire to make them free.
An almost white counterman passes
a waiting brother to serve them first
and the ladies neither notice nor reject
the slighter pleasures of their slavery.
But I who am bound by my mirror
as well as my bed
see causes in colour
as well as sex

and sit here wondering
which me will survive
all these liberations.

❧ From *Othello* (Act 3, Scene 3)

William Shakespeare 1564–1616

Good name in man and woman, dear my lord,
Is the immediate jewel of their souls:
Who steals my purse steals trash; this something, nothing;
Twas mine, tis his, and has been slaves to thousands;
But he that filches from me my good name
Robs me of that which not enriches him
And makes me poor indeed.

❧ To You

Walt Whitman 1819–1892

STRANGER! if you, passing, meet me, and desire to
   speak to me, why should you not speak to me?
And why should I not speak to you?

❧ Words from the Front

Ron Padgett 1942–

We don't look as young
as we used to
except in the dim light
especially in
the soft warmth of candlelight
when we say
in all sincerity
You're so cute
and
You're my cutie.
Imagine
two old people
behaving like this.
It's enough
to make you happy.

❧ Little Prayer

Danez Smith 1989–

let ruin end here

let him find honey
where there was once a slaughter

let him enter the lion's cage
& find a field of lilacs

let this be the healing
& if not let it be

ᨘ Invictus

William Ernest Henley 1849–1903

Out of the night that covers me,
  Black as the pit from pole to pole,
I thank whatever gods may be
  For my unconquerable soul.

In the fell clutch of circumstance
  I have not winced nor cried aloud.
Under the bludgeonings of chance
  My head is bloody, but unbowed.

Beyond this place of wrath and tears
  Looms but the Horror of the shade,
And yet the menace of the years
  Finds and shall find me unafraid.

It matters not how strait the gate,
  How charged with punishments the scroll,
I am the master of my fate,
  I am the captain of my soul.

৯ A Psalm of Life

Henry Wadsworth Longfellow 1807–1882

What The Heart Of The Young Man Said To The Psalmist.

Tell me not, in mournful numbers,
    Life is but an empty dream!
For the soul is dead that slumbers,
    And things are not what they seem.

Life is real! Life is earnest!
    And the grave is not its goal;
Dust thou art, to dust returnest,
    Was not spoken of the soul.

Not enjoyment, and not sorrow,
    Is our destined end or way;
But to act, that each to-morrow
    Find us farther than to-day.

Art is long, and Time is fleeting,
    And our hearts, though stout and brave,
Still, like muffled drums, are beating
    Funeral marches to the grave.

In the world's broad field of battle,
    In the bivouac of Life,
Be not like dumb, driven cattle!
    Be a hero in the strife!

Trust no Future, howe'er pleasant!
  Let the dead Past bury its dead!
Act,—act in the living Present!
  Heart within, and God o'erhead!

Lives of great men all remind us
  We can make our lives sublime,
And, departing, leave behind us
  Footprints on the sands of time;

Footprints, that perhaps another,
  Sailing o'er life's solemn main,
A forlorn and shipwrecked brother,
  Seeing, shall take heart again.

Let us, then, be up and doing,
  With a heart for any fate;
Still achieving, still pursuing,
  Learn to labor and to wait.

❧ If

Rudyard Kipling 1865–1936

If you can keep your head when all about you
    Are losing theirs and blaming it on you,
If you can trust yourself when all men doubt you,
    But make allowance for their doubting too;
If you can wait and not be tired by waiting,
    Or being lied about, don't deal in lies,
Or being hated, don't give way to hating,
    And yet don't look too good, nor talk too wise:

If you can dream—and not make dreams your master;
    If you can think—and not make thoughts your aim;
If you can meet with Triumph and Disaster
    And treat those two impostors just the same;
If you can bear to hear the truth you've spoken
    Twisted by knaves to make a trap for fools,
Or watch the things you gave your life to, broken,
    And stoop and build 'em up with worn-out tools:

If you can make one heap of all your winnings
    And risk it on one turn of pitch-and-toss,
And lose, and start again at your beginnings
    And never breathe a word about your loss;
If you can force your heart and nerve and sinew
    To serve your turn long after they are gone,
And so hold on when there is nothing in you
    Except the Will which says to them: 'Hold on!'

If you can talk with crowds and keep your virtue,
 Or walk with Kings—nor lose the common touch,
If neither foes nor loving friends can hurt you,
 If all men count with you, but none too much;
If you can fill the unforgiving minute
 With sixty seconds' worth of distance run,
Yours is the Earth and everything that's in it,
 And—which is more—you'll be a Man, my son!

ᚱ Men Say They Know Many Things

Henry David Thoreau 1817–1862

Men say they know many things;
But lo! They have taken wings,—
The arts and the sciences,
And a thousand appliances;
The wind that blows
Is all that anybody knows.

❧ Be Like The Bird

Victor Hugo 1802–1885

Be like the bird, who
Pausing in his flight
On a limb too slight
Feels it bend beneath him
Yet sings,
Knowing he has wings.

🐚 The Tables Turned

William Wordsworth 1770–1850

Up! up! my Friend, and quit your books;
Or surely you'll grow double:
Up! up! my Friend, and clear your looks;
Why all this toil and trouble?

The sun above the mountain's head,
A freshening lustre mellow
Through all the long green fields has spread,
His first sweet evening yellow.

Books! 'tis a dull and endless strife:
Come, hear the woodland linnet,
How sweet his music! on my life,
There's more of wisdom in it.

And hark! how blithe the throstle sings!
He, too, is no mean preacher:
Come forth into the light of things,
Let Nature be your teacher.

She has a world of ready wealth,
Our minds and hearts to bless—
Spontaneous wisdom breathed by health,
Truth breathed by cheerfulness.

One impulse from a vernal wood
May teach you more of man,
Of moral evil and of good,
Than all the sages can.

Sweet is the lore which Nature brings;
Our meddling intellect
Mis-shapes the beauteous forms of things:—
We murder to dissect.

Enough of Science and of Art;
Close up those barren leaves;
Come forth, and bring with you a heart
That watches and receives.

❧ The Oak

Alfred, Lord Tennyson 1809–1892

Live thy Life,
   Young and old,
Like yon oak,
Bright in spring,
   Living gold;

Summer-rich
   Then; and then
Autumn-changed,
Soberer-hued
   Gold again.

All his leaves
   Fallen at length,
Look, he stands,
Trunk and bough,
   Naked strength.

❧ The Road Not Taken

Robert Frost 1874–1963

Two roads diverged in a yellow wood,
And sorry I could not travel both
And be one traveler, long I stood
And looked down one as far as I could
To where it bent in the undergrowth;

Then took the other, as just as fair,
And having perhaps the better claim,
Because it was grassy and wanted wear;
Though as for that the passing there
Had worn them really about the same,

And both that morning equally lay
In leaves no step had trodden black.
Oh, I kept the first for another day!
Yet knowing how way leads on to way,
I doubted if I should ever come back.

I shall be telling this with a sigh
Somewhere ages and ages hence:
Two roads diverged in a wood, and I—
I took the one less traveled by,
And that has made all the difference.

❧ Nothing Gold Can Stay

Robert Frost 1874–1963

Nature's first green is gold,
Her hardest hue to hold.
Her early leaf's a flower;
But only so an hour.
Then leaf subsides to leaf.
So Eden sank to grief,
So dawn goes down to day.
Nothing gold can stay.

❧ Past, Present, Future

Emily Brontë 1818–1848

Tell me, tell me, smiling child,
What the past is like to thee?
'An Autumn evening soft and mild
With a wind that sighs mournfully.'

Tell me, what is the present hour?
'A green and flowery spray
Where a young bird sits gathering its power
To mount and fly away.'

And what is the future, happy one?
'A sea beneath a cloudless sun;
A mighty, glorious, dazzling sea
Stretching into infinity.'

❧ Think Not All Is Over

Harriet Beecher Stowe 1811–1896

Think not, when the wailing winds of autumn
Drive the shivering leaflets from the tree,—
Think not all is over: spring returneth,
Buds and leaves and blossoms thou shalt see.

Think not, when the earth lies cold and sealed,
And the weary birds above her mourn,—
Think not all is over: God still liveth,
Songs and sunshine shall again return.

Think not, when thy heart is waste and dreary,
When thy cherished hopes lie chill and sere,—
Think not all is over: God still loveth,
He will wipe away thy every tear.

Weeping for a night alone endureth,
God at last shall bring a morning hour;
In the frozen buds of every winter
Sleep the blossoms of a future flower.

❧ Ozymandias

Percy Bysshe Shelley 1792–1822

I met a traveller from an antique land,
Who said—"Two vast and trunkless legs of stone
Stand in the desert. . . . Near them, on the sand,
Half sunk a shattered visage lies, whose frown,
And wrinkled lip, and sneer of cold command,
Tell that its sculptor well those passions read
Which yet survive, stamped on these lifeless things,
The hand that mocked them, and the heart that fed;
And on the pedestal, these words appear:
My name is Ozymandias, King of Kings;
Look on my Works, ye Mighty, and despair!
Nothing beside remains. Round the decay
Of that colossal Wreck, boundless and bare
The lone and level sands stretch far away."

❧ Do not go gentle into that good night

Dylan Thomas 1914–1953

Do not go gentle into that good night,
Old age should burn and rave at close of day;
Rage, rage against the dying of the light.

Though wise men at their end know dark is right,
Because their words had forked no lightning they
Do not go gentle into that good night.

Good men, the last wave by, crying how bright
Their frail deeds might have danced in a green bay,
Rage, rage against the dying of the light.

Wild men who caught and sang the sun in flight,
And learn, too late, they grieved it on its way,
Do not go gentle into that good night.

Grave men, near death, who see with blinding sight
Blind eyes could blaze like meteors and be gay,
Rage, rage against the dying of the light.

And you, my father, there on the sad height,
Curse, bless, me now with your fierce tears, I pray.
Do not go gentle into that good night.
Rage, rage against the dying of the light.

❧ Leisure

W.H. Davies 1871–1940

What is this life if, full of care,
We have no time to stand and stare?-

No time to stand beneath the boughs
And stare as long as sheep or cows:

No time to see, when woods we pass,
Where squirrels hide their nuts in grass:

No time to see, in broad daylight,
Streams full of stars, like skies at night:

No time to turn at Beauty's glance,
And watch her feet, how they can dance:

No time to wait till her mouth can
Enrich that smile her eyes began?

A poor life this if, full of care,
We have no time to stand and stare.

🐦 *From* Ye Wearie Wayfarer (Fytte 8)

Adam Lindsay Gordon 1833–1870

Life is mostly froth and bubble,
Two things stand like stone,
Kindness in another's trouble,
Courage in your own.

❧ Self-pity

D.H. Lawrence 1885–1930

I never saw a wild thing
sorry for itself.
A small bird will drop frozen dead from a bough
without ever having felt sorry for itself.

❧ The Word

Tony Hoagland 1953–2018

Down near the bottom
of the crossed-out list
of things you have to do today,

between "green thread"
and "broccoli," you find
that you have penciled "sunlight."

Resting on the page, the word
is as beautiful. It touches you
as if you had a friend

and sunlight were a present
he had sent you from someplace distant
as this morning—to cheer you up,

and to remind you that,
among your duties, pleasure
is a thing

that also needs accomplishing
Do you remember?
that time and light are kinds

of love, and love
is no less practical
than a coffee grinder

or a safe spare tire?
Tomorrow you may be utterly
without a clue,

but today you get a telegram
from the heart in exile,
proclaiming that the kingdom

still exists,
the king and queen alive,
still speaking to their children,

—to any one among them
who can find the time,
to sit out in the sun and listen.

❧ Advice

Langston Hughes 1901–1967

Folks, I'm telling you,
birthing is hard
and dying is mean—
so get yourself
a little loving
in between.

October

Contemplation

O CTOBER was known as 'Winterfylleth' by the Anglo-Saxons
– 'Winter Full Moon.' It was a time to mark and celebrate
the onset of winter, the season when the nights outlast the
days. It is a month of darkening evenings spent indoors, and nights
filled with the sound of our own ruminations. Sometimes this can be a
gift. But long, contemplative evenings sometimes become sleepless
nights, lying awake with worried thoughts at three o'clock in the
morning. In times like these, a poem by the bedside can offer a source
of solace.

Reading poetry encourages quiet reflection. The month begins with
Emily Dickinson, whose poetry in general is very contemplative. Her
stylistic experimentation, aiming to make abstract ideas concrete and
tangible, contributed to her standing as one of America's greatest poets.
And all this despite her avoidance of publication, preferring to send
her poems back and forth privately amongst friends. Her family discov-
ered nearly two thousand poems after her death, hidden in hand-sewn
notebooks. They were all eventually published to great acclaim. Perhaps
her sister, who published Dickinson's work posthumously, was aware
that it is not enough for a poet to simply write; a poem is nothing
without you, the reader.

Here, Dickinson reminds us to quiet our thoughts: 'How happy is the little stone / That rambles in the road alone, / And doesn't care about careers, / And exigencies never fears.' Her implied comparison between the mind of a stone and of a person presents well-worn advice – that if we could worry less, we might be happier – through an entirely unfamiliar lens, to force us to truly think about it. Yet other poets operate along different lines. Piet Hein's pithy 'Thoughts on a Station Platform' gives similar advice through the medium of the all-too-familiar predicament of a frustrated commuter in an epigrammatic tone.

Also featured is Joy Harjo, whose poem 'Remember' is a brilliant example of how new voices help us contemplate new perspectives. As the US' first Poet Laureate with an Indigenous American background, Harjo is an important figure in the Native American Renaissance in Literature. She infuses her poetry with her Muscogee Nation heritage and the attendant belief in the unity between all things: 'Remember you are this universe and this / universe is you.' An emphasis on connection is often how the poets offer comfort in our worries and remind us we are not alone.

Sleep, so easy for some and yet so difficult to achieve in anxious times, has been addressed by plenty of poets: we all want to 'sleep as [we] in childhood sweetly slept,' as John Clare puts it. Romantic master-pieces by William Wordsworth and John Keats accompany Clare's insomniac poem, while Gerard Manley Hopkins' lines, 'What hours, O what black hours we have spent / This night', are the perfect example of how poetry can help harmonise our sadness.

The contemporary poets Meg Cox and Carol Ann Duffy both touch on the radio, illuminating the human urge to fill the empty nights with the company of sound – which Duffy terms 'the radio's prayer'. Cox's 'Awake at Night' describes how, 'listening to the World Service', she 'heard a man explain he wasn't lonely; / he talked to his dead wife all the time / although he knew she wasn't there'. Despite its empathy, hers is a pragmatic poetry, and her unsentimental ending almost invites us to smile at her misfortune – and perhaps, in turn, our own.

Elizabeth Bishop finds comfort in solitude through the 'world inverted', 'where the shadows are really the body': 'The moon in the bureau mirror / looks out a million miles.' 'Far away and beyond sleep,' the moon accompanies us through restless nights. T.E. Hulme's description of a night-time walk in 'Autumn' also personifies the moon, relaying how he 'saw the ruddy moon lean over a hedge / Like a red-faced farmer'.

Sometimes, the role of the poet is simply to lull us to sleep, as with William Blake's 'Cradle Song' and its soothing, gentle rhymes: 'Sleep, sleep; in thy sleep / Little sorrows sit and weep.' So too with Char March's modern lullaby, where she draws out a seascape from sleepless nights; 'wave a flipper / at a shoal of passing thoughts / snooze for a brief dream / of mackerel.'

In times of sadness or worry, a poem can remind us to contemplate the good things and find moments of beauty or joy. Paul Laurence Dunbar's poem 'Sympathy' uses a caged bird's singing to represent hopeful resistance in the face of hardship and oppressive conditions; 'It is not a carol of joy or glee, / But a prayer that he sends up from his heart's deep core.' Leigh Hunt's 'Rondeau' is a reminder that past joys can never be undone, and are a store of happiness for us to reflect on: 'Say I'm weary, say I'm sad, / Say that health and wealth have missed me, / Sad I'm growing old, but add, / Jenny kissed me.' Amy Levy can find beauty even in the 'slow, creeping weariness' and 'drowsy blankness of the mind' that accompanies a 'dog-tired' evening.

Elsewhere, the poets reassure us – if only with the sound and the rhythm of their voice, as in W.H. Auden's tender villanelle on the passage of time: 'The winds must come from somewhere when they blow, / There must be reasons why the leaves decay; / Time will say nothing but I told you so.' Amy Lowell, on the other hand, inspires us to find peace in the beauty of the outdoors. For Lowell, autumn is not a time when nature withers and the leaves 'decay', but a time when trees shedding their leaves is almost an art, if only we can pause to enjoy it. Night is not a time of darkness, but of 'moonlight' which leaves each leaf 'fringed with silver'.

But the poets always seem to return to the point that we ought not to let contemplation descend into panic. Pushkin's soothing promise,

'Tis but a moment, all will pass', is echoed by Penelope Shuttle's anecdotal offering of hope that things may yet improve: 'Even thinking about unpaid bills / doesn't make me weep, / though I used to weep and weep.' And finally, the month ends with the great Irish poet Derek Mahon's promise that 'Everything is going to be all right'.

The sun rises in spite of everything
And the far cities are beautiful and bright

Derek Mahon

❧ How happy is the little stone

Emily Dickinson 1830–1886

How happy is the little Stone
That rambles in the Road alone,
And does'nt care about Careers
And Exigencies never fears –
Whose Coat of elemental Brown
A passing Universe put on,
And independent as the sun,
Associates or glows alone,
Fulfilling absolute Decree
In casual simplicity –

❧ Thoughts on a Station Platform

Piet Hein 1905–1996

It ought to be plain
how little you gain
by getting excited
and vexed.

You'll always be late
for the previous train,
and always on time
for the next.

?❧ The Coming of Good Luck

Robert Herrick 1591–1674

So Good-luck came, and on my roofe did light,
Like noyse-lesse Snow; or as the dew of night:
Not all at once, but gently, as the trees
Are, by the Sun-beams, tickel'd by degrees.

❧ Remember

Joy Harjo 1951–

Remember the sky that you were born under,
know each of the star's stories.
Remember the moon, know who she is.
Remember the sun's birth at dawn, that is the
strongest point of time. Remember sundown
and the giving away to night.
Remember your birth, how your mother struggled
to give you form and breath. You are evidence of
her life, and her mother's, and hers.
Remember your father. He is your life, also.
Remember the earth whose skin you are:
red earth, black earth, yellow earth, white earth
brown earth, we are earth.
Remember the plants, trees, animal life who all have their
tribes, their families, their histories, too. Talk to them,
listen to them. They are alive poems.
Remember the wind. Remember her voice. She knows the
origin of this universe.
Remember you are all people and all people
are you.
Remember you are this universe and this
universe is you.
Remember all is in motion, is growing, is you.
Remember language comes from this.
Remember the dance language is, that life is.
Remember.

ᣟ If I Could Tell You

W.H. Auden 1907–1973

Time will say nothing but I told you so,
Time only knows the price we have to pay;
If I could tell you I would let you know.

If we should weep when clowns put on their show,
If we should stumble when musicians play,
Time will say nothing but I told you so.

There are no fortunes to be told, although,
Because I love you more than I can say,
If I could tell you I would let you know.

The winds must come from somewhere when they blow,
There must be reasons why the leaves decay;
Time will say nothing but I told you so.

Perhaps the roses really want to grow,
The vision seriously intends to stay;
If I could tell you I would let you know.

Suppose all the lions get up and go,
And all the brooks and soldiers run away;
Will Time say nothing but I told you so?
If I could tell you I would let you know.

❧ I wake and feel the fell of dark, not day

Gerard Manley Hopkins 1844–1889

I wake and feel the fell of dark, not day.
What hours, O what black hours we have spent
This night! what sights you, heart, saw; ways you went!
And more must, in yet longer light's delay.
    With witness I speak this. But where I say
Hours I mean years, mean life. And my lament
Is cries countless, cries like dead letters sent
To dearest him that lives alas! away.

    I am gall, I am heartburn. God's most deep decree
Bitter would have me taste: my taste was me;
Bones built in me, flesh filled, blood brimmed the curse.
    Selfyeast of spirit a dull dough sours. I see
The lost are like this, and their scourge to be
As I am mine, their sweating selves; but worse.

ॐ Rondeau

Leigh Hunt 1784–1859

Jenny kissed me when we met,
   Jumping from the chair she sat in;
Time, you thief, who love to get
   Sweets into your list, put that in:
Say I'm weary, say I'm sad,
   Say that health and wealth have missed me,
Say I'm growing old, but add,
   Jenny kissed me.

❧ If I Can Stop One Heart from Breaking

Emily Dickinson 1830–1886

If I can stop one Heart from breaking
I shall not live in vain
If I can ease one Life the Aching,
Or cool one Pain,

Or help one fainting Robin
Unto his Nest again
I shall not live in vain.

❧ Count That Day Lost

George Eliot 1819–1880

If you sit down at set of sun
And count the acts that you have done,
And, counting, find
One self-denying deed, one word
That eased the heart of him who heard,
One glance most kind
That fell like sunshine where it went—
Then you may count that day well spent.

But if, through all the livelong day,
You've cheered no heart, by yea or nay—
If, through it all
You've nothing done that you can trace
That brought the sunshine to one face—
No act most small
That helped some soul and nothing cost—
Then count that day as worse than lost.

If you sit down at set of sun
And count the acts that you have done,
And, counting, find
One self-denying deed, one word
That eased the heart of him who heard,
One glance most kind
That fell like sunshine where it went—
Then you may count that day well spent.

But if, through all the livelong day,
You've cheered no heart, by yea or nay—
If, through it all
You've nothing done that you can trace
That brought the sunshine to one face—
No act most small
That helped some soul and nothing cost—
Then count that day as worse than lost.

❧ The End of the Day

Amy Levy 1861–1889

Dead-tired, dog-tired, as the vivid day
Fails and slackens and fades away.—
The sky that was so blue before
With sudden clouds is shrouded o'er.
Swiftly, stilly the mists uprise,
Till blurred and grey the landscape lies.

All day we have plied the oar; all day
Eager and keen have said our say
On life and death, on love and art,
On good or ill at Nature's heart.
Now, grown so tired, we scarce can lift
The lazy oars, but onward drift.
And the silence is only stirred
Here and there by a broken word.

O, sweeter far than strain and stress
Is the slow, creeping weariness.
And better far than thought I find
The drowsy blankness of the mind.
More than all joys of soul or sense
Is this divine indifference;
Where grief a shadow grows to be,
And peace a possibility.

❧ The Fury of Rainstorms

Anne Sexton 1928–1974

The rain drums down like red ants,
each bouncing off my window.
The ants are in great pain
and they cry out as they hit
as if their little legs were only
stitched on and their heads pasted.
And oh they bring to mind the grave,
so humble, so willing to be beat upon
with its awful lettering and
the body lying underneath
without an umbrella.
Depression is boring, I think
and I would do better to make
some soup and light up the cave.

❧ I Am!

John Clare 1793–1864

I am—yet what I am none cares or knows;
My friends forsake me like a memory lost:
I am the self-consumer of my woes—
They rise and vanish in oblivious host,
Like shadows in love's frenzied stifled throes
And yet I am, and live—like vapours tossed

Into the nothingness of scorn and noise,
Into the living sea of waking dreams,
Where there is neither sense of life or joys,
But the vast shipwreck of my life's esteems;
Even the dearest that I loved the best
Are strange—nay, rather, stranger than the rest.

I long for scenes where man hath never trod
A place where woman never smiled or wept
There to abide with my Creator, God,
And sleep as I in childhood sweetly slept,
Untroubling and untroubled where I lie
The grass below—above the vaulted sky.

❧ Not Waving but Drowning

Stevie Smith 1902–1971

Nobody heard him, the dead man,
But still he lay moaning:
I was much further out than you thought
And not waving but drowning.

Poor chap, he always loved larking
And now he's dead
It must have been too cold for him his heart gave way,
They said.

Oh, no no no, it was too cold always
(Still the dead one lay moaning)
I was much too far out all my life
And not waving but drowning.

❧ Sympathy

Paul Laurence Dunbar 1872–1906

I know what the caged bird feels, alas!
    When the sun is bright on the upland slopes;
When the wind stirs soft through the springing grass,
And the river flows like a stream of glass;
    When the first bird sings and the first bud opes,
And the faint perfume from its chalice steals—
I know what the caged bird feels!

I know why the caged bird beats his wing
    Till its blood is red on the cruel bars;
For he must fly back to his perch and cling
When he fain would be on the bough a-swing;
    And a pain still throbs in the old, old scars
And they pulse again with a keener sting—
I know why he beats his wing!

I know why the caged bird sings, ah me,
    When his wing is bruised and his bosom sore,—
When he beats his bars and he would be free;
It is not a carol of joy or glee,
    But a prayer that he sends from his heart's deep core,
But a plea, that upward to Heaven he flings—
I know why the caged bird sings!

ॐ The Consolation

Anne Brontë 1820–1849

Though bleak these woods and damp the ground
With fallen leaves so thickly strewn,
And cold the wind that wanders round
With wild and melancholy moan:

There is a friendly roof, I know,
Might shield me from the wintry blast;
There is a fire, whose ruddy glow
Will cheer me for my wanderings past.

And so, though still where'er I go
Cold stranger-glances meet my eye,
Though, when my spirit sinks in woe,
Unheeded swells the unbidden sigh,

Though solitude, endured too long
Bids youthful joys too soon decay,
Makes mirth a stranger to my tongue,
And overclouds my noon of day;

When kindly thoughts that would have way,
Flow back discouraged to my breast;
I know there is, though far away,
A home where heart and soul may rest.

Warm hands are there, that, clasped in mine,
The warmer heart will not belie;
While mirth, and truth, and friendship shine
In smiling lip and earnest eye.

The ice that gathers round my heart
May there be thawed; and sweetly, then,
The joys of youth that now depart,
Will come to cheer my soul again.

Though far I roam, this thought shall be
My hope, my comfort everywhere;
While such a home remains to me,
My heart shall never know despair!

❧ Insomnia

Dante Gabriel Rossetti 1828–1882

Thin are the night-skirts left behind
By daybreak hours that onward creep,
And thin, alas! the shred of sleep
That wavers with the spirit's wind:
But in half-dreams that shift and roll
And still remember and forget,
My soul this hour has drawn your soul
A little nearer yet.

Our lives, most dear, are never near,
Our thoughts are never far apart,
Though all that draws us heart to heart
Seems fainter now and now more clear.
To-night Love claims his full control,
And with desire and with regret
My soul this hour has drawn your soul
A little nearer yet.

Is there a home where heavy earth
Melts to bright air that breathes no pain,
Where water leaves no thirst again
And springing fire is Love's new birth?
If faith long bound to one true goal
May there at length its hope beget,
My soul that hour shall draw your soul
For ever nearer yet.

☙ Lines Written at Night During Insomnia

Alexander Pushkin 1799–1837
Translated by DM Thomas

I can't sleep; no light burns;
All round, darkness, irksome sleep.
Only the monotonous
Ticking of the clock,
The old wives chatter of fate,
Trembling of the sleeping night,
Mouse-like scurrying of life . . .
Why do you disturb me?
What do you mean tedious whispers?
Is it the day I have wasted
Reproaching me or murmuring?
What do you want from me?
Are you calling me or prophesying?
I want to understand you,
I seek a meaning in you . . .

ও To Sleep

William Wordsworth 1770–1850

Fond words have oft been spoken to thee, Sleep!
And thou hast had thy store of tenderest names;
The very sweetest, Fancy culls or frames,
When thankfulness of heart is strong and deep!
Dear Bosom-child we call thee, that dost steep
In rich reward all suffering; Balm that tames
All anguish; Saint that evil thoughts and aims
Takest away, and into souls dost creep,
Like to a breeze from heaven. Shall I alone,
I surely not a man ungently made,
Call thee worst Tyrant by which Flesh is crost?
Perverse, self-willed to own and to disown,
Mere slave of them who never for thee prayed,
Still last to come where thou art wanted most!

❧ Insomnia

Elizabeth Bishop 1911–1979

The moon in the bureau mirror
looks out a million miles
(and perhaps with pride, at herself,
but she never, never smiles)
far and away beyond sleep, or
perhaps she's a daytime sleeper.

By the Universe deserted,
she'd tell it to go to hell,
and she'd find a body of water,
or a mirror, on which to dwell.
So wrap up care in a cobweb
and drop it down the well

into that world inverted
where left is always right,
where the shadows are really the body,
where we stay awake all night,
where the heavens are shallow as the sea
is now deep, and you love me.

❧ Autumn

T.E. Hulme 1883–1917

A touch of cold in the Autumn night—
I walked abroad,
And saw the ruddy moon lean over a hedge
Like a red-faced farmer.
I did not stop to speak, but nodded,
And round about were the wistful stars
With white faces like town children.

❧ Consolation

Robert Louis Stevenson 1850–1894

Though he, that ever kind and true,
Kept stoutly step by step with you,
Your whole long, gusty lifetime through,
Be gone a while before,
Be now a moment gone before,
Yet, doubt not, soon the seasons shall restore
Your friend to you.

He has but turned the corner—still
He pushes on with right good will,
Through mire and marsh, by heugh and hill,
That self-same arduous way—
That self-same upland, hopeful way,
That you and he through many a doubtful day
Attempted still.

He is not dead, this friend—not dead,
But in the path we mortals tread
Got some few, trifling steps ahead
And nearer to the end;
So that you too, once past the bend,
Shall meet again, as face to face, this friend
You fancy dead.

Push gaily on, strong heart! The while
You travel forward mile by mile,
He loiters with a backward smile
Till you can overtake,
And strains his eyes to search his wake,
Or whistling, as he sees you through the brake,
Waits on a stile.

❧ A Clear Midnight

Walt Whitman 1819–1892

This is thy hour O Soul, thy free flight into the wordless,
Away from books, away from art, the day erased, the
lesson done,
Thee fully forth emerging, silent, gazing, pondering the
themes thou lovest best,
Night, sleep, death and the stars.

❧ Autumn

Amy Lowell 1874–1925

All day I have watched the purple vine leaves
Fall into the water.
And now in the moonlight they still fall,
But each leaf is fringed with silver.

❧ Awake at Night

Meg Cox 1944–

and listening to the World Service
(one benefit of sleeping on my own)
I heard a man explain he wasn't lonely;
he talked to his dead wife all the time
although he knew she wasn't there.

He told her about things she would once
have liked, and still did, according to him.
He asked her advice about the children
but didn't say if what she said was any help.

As I drifted off to sleep I wondered
if I could do that too – talk to him.
But when your own dear departed
is still living with his wife in Wembley
it's just not the same.

❧ Prayer

Carol Ann Duffy 1955–

Some days, although we cannot pray, a prayer
utters itself. So, a woman will lift
her head from the sieve of her hands and stare
at the minims sung by a tree, a sudden gift.

Some nights, although we are faithless, the truth
enters our hearts, that small familiar pain;
then a man will stand stock-still, hearing his youth
in the distant Latin chanting of a train.

Pray for us now. Grade I piano scales
console the lodger looking out across
a Midlands town. Then dusk, and someone calls
a child's name as though they named their loss.

Darkness outside. Inside, the radio's prayer—
Rockall. Malin. Dogger. Finisterre.

❧ Insomnia has had a very bad press
Char March 1961–

but, imagine yourself
a large, grey seal:
bob up for air
rise and fall with the swell
of deep-night
when all sounds
are strange, distorted,
and your whiskered snout
radars through fug and fog.

now dive into shallow
then deeper sleep,
turn your dappled belly up
wave a flipper
at a shoal of passing thoughts
snooze for a brief dream
of mackerel,
then rise in a stream of bubbles
to take the air again.

❧ Cradle Song

William Blake 1757–1827

Sleep, sleep, beauty bright,
Dreaming in the joys of night;
Sleep, sleep; in thy sleep
Little sorrows sit and weep.

Sweet babe, in thy face
Soft desires I can trace,
Secret joys and secret smiles,
Little pretty infant wiles.

As thy softest limbs I feel
Smiles as of the morning steal
O'er thy cheek, and o'er thy breast
Where thy little heart doth rest.

O the cunning wiles that creep
In thy little heart asleep!
When thy little heart doth wake,
Then the dreadful night shall break.

❧ To Sleep

John Keats 1795–1821

O soft embalmer of the still midnight,
  Shutting, with careful fingers and benign,
Our gloom-pleas'd eyes, embower'd from the light,
  Enshaded in forgetfulness divine:
O soothest Sleep! if so it please thee, close
  In midst of this thine hymn my willing eyes,
Or wait the "Amen," ere thy poppy throws
  Around my bed its lulling charities.
Then save me, or the passed day will shine
Upon my pillow, breeding many woes,—
  Save me from curious Conscience, that still lords
Its strength for darkness, burrowing like a mole;
  Turn the key deftly in the oiled wards,
And seal the hushed Casket of my Soul.

❧ Before Dawn

Penelope Shuttle 1947–

I used to wake early, and weep.
Now I wake just as early,
calm as a cloud
in the moony sky outside.
Even thinking about unpaid bills
doesn't make me weep,
though I used to weep and weep.

4.30 a.m. No way of getting back
to sleep so I listen in
to the silence of a world dark and at rest.
I know other women
wider-awake than me.
I hear the silence beyond their weeping,
streetlamps outside their windows
won't blank out for hours and hours yet.

I used to wake early, etc . . .
Now I let my old friend Sleep
go his own sweet way,
listen to whoever is wide-awake in me,
running the flats of her hands
over the rough walls of the world,
looking for what?
A way in? A way out?
You tell me.

❧ Consolation

Alexander Pushkin 1799–1837
Translated by Ivan Panin

Life,—does it disappoint thee?
Grieve not, nor be angry thou!
In days of sorrow gentle be:
Come shall, believe, the joyful day.

In the future lives the heart:
Is the present sad indeed?
'Tis but a moment, all will pass;
Once in the past, it shall be dear.

❧ Everything Is Going To Be All Right

Derek Mahon 1941–2020

How should I not be glad to contemplate
the clouds clearing beyond the dormer window
and a high tide reflected on the ceiling?
There will be dying, there will be dying,
but there is no need to go into that.
The lines flow from the hand unbidden
and the hidden source is the watchful heart.
The sun rises in spite of everything
and the far cities are beautiful and bright.
I lie here in a riot of sunlight
watching the day break and the clouds flying.
Everything is going to be all right.

November

Endings

As the days get darker and colder, November sees nature wither. In the Western world it has been marked since pagan times as a month when the dead are honoured. The ancient Greek myth of Persephone's abduction by Hades, the god of the dead and the king of the Underworld, directly associates the onset of winter with the themes of mourning and remembrance. Persephone's mother, Demeter, is the goddess of agriculture, and because Persephone must split the year between Earth and the Underworld, Demeter refuses to let plants grow in the time that she is gone; hence winters are born.

The association between the winter and ending seems to be universally human. At the start of November the ancient Celts celebrated Samhain, a death festival when one would leave out food for their ancestor's returning souls. Today the same time is marked by Christianity's All Soul's Day and the Mexican Day of the Dead, encouraging joyful celebration of the departed. And in 1816 when Germany introduced Totensonntag ('Sunday of the Dead'), it was placed in November, towards the end of the month.

In many of the world's remembrance festivals, both now and in the past, there has been an implicit assumption that people would return from the afterlife – as though it has always been part of our human inheritance to feel that remembering could be enough to keep someone alive. The ability of the great poets to speak to us long after they have passed offers a similarly powerful message of hope, reminding us that the person need not end with their life; that memory can resist all endings. Even once a poet, or indeed any person, is gone, they can hold our hands across the world, across time, and remind us that we are never alone.

Of course, there are other types of ending aside from the passage of life to death. Poetry helps us navigate the complexities of endings, offering wisdom, consolation and solace. Whether we are experiencing the end of a friendship, a life, a love affair, or simply approaching the autumn of our years, poetry provides a guiding light through these challenging times.

Whether we embrace or mourn an ending, the feelings evoked by absence, loss and impermanence are never easy to express – the poets offer a shared language to describe our emotions, providing comfort and understanding when it is most needed. For whichever type of ending we experience, W.S. Merwin's depiction of loss offers a profound explanation for how overwhelming our loneliness can be: 'Everything I do is stitched with its color.' And hence the poets soothe us, even if only by sharing our distress and granting us the freedom to feel. Certainly this is the case with Andrea Cohen, whose candid 'Refusal to Mourn' voices the precise feelings we feel most strongly we need to suppress; in a completely different way, Wendy Cope's characteristically comic musing on her own funeral takes an irreverent look at our mourning rituals: 'If you are asked to talk about me for five minutes, please do not go on for eight. / There is a strict timetable at the crematorium and nobody wants to be late.'

At the same time, autumn's falling leaves and fading colours draw our attention to all that is impermanent, and remind us that endings are natural. For Shakespeare, the greatest of poets, both autumn and dusk become metaphors for death's slow approach: 'In me thou see'st the twilight of such day / As after sunset faded in the west, / Which by and by black night doth take away, / Death's second self, that seals up all in rest.' Life and death are repositioned as simply being two aspects of nature, like day and night, and none of this needs to cause us pain: 'This thou perceiv'st, which makes thy love more strong, / To love that well which thou must leave ere long.' His message is clear – the fact of death ought only to renew our enthusiasm for life; the fact of loss ought only make us love more strongly. With the year drawing to a close, November is a time to reflect on what has passed and what has changed, and to explore the role of endings in our lives.

The month concludes with wisdom from Scotland's fourth Makar (poet laureate), Kathleen Jamie, whose prose poem offers the promise of hope in its own profound ending: 'To be healed is not to be saved from mortality, but rather, released back into it: we are returned to the wild, into possibilities for ageing and change.'

Better by far you should forget and smile
Than that you should remember and be sad.

Christina Rossetti

❧ There's Nothing Like the Sun

Edward Thomas 1878–1917

There's nothing like the sun as the year dies,
   Kind as it can be, this world being made so,
To stones and men and beasts and birds and flies,
To all things that it touches except snow,
   Whether on mountains side or street of town.
The south wall warms me: November has begun,
   Yet never shone the sun as fair as now
While the sweet last-left damsons from the bough
With spangles of the morning's storm drop down
   Because the starling shakes it, whistling what
Once swallows sang. But I have not forgot
That there is nothing, too, like March's sun,
Like April's, or July's, or June's, or May's,
Or January's, or February's, great days:
August, September, October, and December
Have equal days, all different from November.
No day of any month but I have said—
Or, if I could live long enough, should say—
'There's nothing like the sun that shines today.'
There's nothing like the sun till we are dead.

❧ When You Are Old

W.B. Yeats 1865–1939

When you are old and grey and full of sleep,
And nodding by the fire, take down this book,
And slowly read, and dream of the soft look
Your eyes had once, and of their shadows deep;

How many loved your moments of glad grace,
And loved your beauty with love false or true,
But one man loved the pilgrim soul in you,
And loved the sorrows of your changing face;

And bending down beside the glowing bars,
Murmur, a little sadly, how Love fled
And paced upon the mountains overhead
And hid his face amid a crowd of stars.

❧ Shake Hands

A.E. Housman 1859–1936

Shake hands, we shall never be friends, all's over;
    I only vex you the more I try.
All's wrong that ever I've done or said,
And nought to help it in this dull head:
    Shake hands, here's luck, good-bye.

But if you come to a road where danger
    Or guilt or anguish or shame's to share,
Be good to the lad that loves you true
And the soul that was born to die for you,
    And whistle and I'll be there.

So We'll Go No More a Roving

Lord Byron 1788–1824

So, we'll go no more a roving
  So late into the night,
Though the heart be still as loving,
  And the moon be still as bright.

For the sword outwears its sheath,
  And the soul wears out the breast,
And the heart must pause to breathe,
  And love itself have rest.

Though the night was made for loving,
  And the day returns too soon,
Yet we'll go no more a roving
  By the light of the moon.

❧ Ebb

Edna St. Vincent Millay 1892–1950

I know what my heart is like
  Since your love died:
It is like a hollow ledge
Holding a little pool
  Left there by the tide,
  A little tepid pool,
Drying inward from the edge.

❦ Separation

W.S. Merwin 1927–2019

Your absence has gone through me
Like thread through a needle.
Everything I do is stitched with its color.

❧ After Love

Sara Teasdale 1884–1933

There is no magic any more,
   We meet as other people do,
You work no miracle for me
   Nor I for you.

You were the wind and I the sea—
   There is no splendor any more,
I have grown listless as the pool
   Beside the shore.

But though the pool is safe from storm
   And from the tide has found surcease,
It grows more bitter than the sea,
   For all its peace.

❧ Sonnet 73

William Shakespeare 1564–1616

That time of year thou mayst in me behold
When yellow leaves, or none, or few, do hang
Upon those boughs which shake against the cold,
Bare ruin'd choirs, where late the sweet birds sang.
In me thou see'st the twilight of such day
As after sunset fadeth in the west,
Which by and by black night doth take away,
Death's second self, that seals up all in rest.
In me thou see'st the glowing of such fire
That on the ashes of his youth doth lie,
As the death-bed whereon it must expire,
Consum'd with that which it was nourish'd by.
This thou perceiv'st, which makes thy love more strong,
To love that well which thou must leave ere long.

❧ The Snow Fairy

Claude McKay 1890–1948

I

Throughout the afternoon I watched them there,
Snow-fairies falling, falling from the sky,
Whirling fantastic in the misty air,
Contending fierce for space supremacy.
And they flew down a mightier force at night,
As though in heaven there was revolt and riot,
And they, frail things had taken panic flight
Down to the calm earth seeking peace and quiet.
I went to bed and rose at early dawn
To see them huddled together in a heap,
Each merged into the other upon the lawn,
Worn out by the sharp struggle, fast asleep.
The sun shone brightly on them half the day,
By night they stealthily had stol'n away.

II

And suddenly my thoughts then turned to you
Who came to me upon a winter's night,
When snow-sprites round my attic window flew,
Your hair disheveled, eyes aglow with light.
My heart was like the weather when you came,
The wanton winds were blowing loud and long;
But you, with joy and passion all aflame,
You danced and sang a lilting summer song.
I made room for you in my little bed,
Took covers from the closet fresh and warm,
A downful pillow for your scented head,
And lay down with you resting in my arm.
You went with Dawn. You left me ere the day,
The lonely actor of a dreamy play.

☙ Atantis – A Lost Sonnet

Eavan Boland 1944–2020

How on earth did it happen, I used to wonder
that a whole city—arches, pillars, colonnades,
not to mention vehicles and animals—had all
one fine day gone under?

I mean, I said to myself, the world was small then.
Surely a great city must have been missed?
I miss our old city—

white pepper, white pudding, you and I meeting
under fanlights and low skies to go home in it.
Maybe what really happened is

this: the old fable-makers searched hard for a word
to convey that what is gone is gone forever and
never found it. And so, in the best traditions of

where we come from, they gave their sorrow a name
and drowned it.

❧ Music, when soft voices die

Percy Bysshe Shelley 1792–1822

Music, when soft voices die,
Vibrates in the memory—
Odours, when sweet violets sicken,
Live within the sense they quicken.

Rose leaves, when the rose is dead,
Are heaped for the belovèd's bed;
And so thy thoughts, when thou art gone,
Love itself shall slumber on.

❧ The Last Performance

Thomas Hardy 1840–1928

"I am playing my oldest tunes," declared she,
    "All the old tunes I know,—
Those I learnt ever so long ago."
—Why she should think just then she'd play them
    Silence cloaks like snow.

When I returned from the town at nightfall
    Notes continued to pour
As when I had left two hours before:
"It's the very last time," she said in closing;
    "From now I play no more."

A few morns onward found her fading,
    And, as her life outflew,
I thought of her playing her tunes right through;
And I felt she had known of what was coming,
    And wondered how she knew.

❧ Going without Saying

Bernard O'Donoghue 1945–

i.m. Joe Flynn

It is a great pity we don't know
When the dead are going to die
So that, over a last companionable
Drink, we could tell them
How much we liked them.

Happy the man who, dying, can
Place his hand on his heart and say:
'At least I didn't neglect to tell
The thrush how beautifully she sings.'

❧ Hold out your arms

Helen Dunmore 1952–2017

Death, hold out your arms for me
Embrace me
Give me your motherly caress,
Through all this suffering
You have not forgotten me.

You are the bearded iris that bakes its rhizomes
Beside the wall,
Your scent flushes with loveliness,
Sherbet, pure iris
Lovely and intricate.

I am the child who stands by the wall
Not much taller than the iris.
The sun covers me
The day waits for me
In my funny dress.

Death, you heap into my arms
A basket of unripe damsons
Red crisscross straps that button behind me.
I don't know about school,
My knowledge is for papery bud covers
Tall stems and brown
Bees touching here and there, delicately
Before a swerve to the sun.

Death stoops over me
Her long skirts slide,
She knows I am shy.
Even the puffed sleeves on my white blouse
Embarrass me,
She will pick me up and hold me
So no one can see me,
I will scrub my hair into hers.

There, the iris increases
Note by note
As the wall gives back heat.
Death, there's no need to ask:
A mother will always lift a child
As a rhizome
Must lift up a flower
So you settle me
My arms twining,
Thighs gripping your hips
Where the swell of you is.

As you push back my hair
– Which could do with a comb
But never mind –
You murmur
'We're nearly there.'

❧ Late Fragment

Raymond Carver 1938–1988

And did you get what
you wanted from this life, even so?
I did.
And what did you want?
To call myself beloved, to feel myself
beloved on the earth.

Funeral Blues (Stop all the clocks)

W.H. Auden 1907–1973

Stop all the clocks, cut off the telephone,
Prevent the dog from barking with a juicy bone,
Silence the pianos and with muffled drum
Bring out the coffin, let the mourners come.

Let aeroplanes circle moaning overhead
Scribbling on the sky the message He Is Dead,
Put crêpe bows round the white necks of the public doves,
Let the traffic policemen wear black cotton gloves.

He was my North, my South, my East and West,
My working week and my Sunday rest,
My noon, my midnight, my talk, my song;
I thought that love would last for ever: I was wrong.

The stars are not wanted now: put out every one;
Pack up the moon and dismantle the sun;
Pour away the ocean and sweep up the wood;
For nothing now can ever come to any good.

❧ Remember

Christina Rossetti 1830–1894

Remember me when I am gone away,
  Gone far away into the silent land;
  When you can no more hold me by the hand,
Nor I half turn to go yet turning stay.
Remember me when no more day by day
  You tell me of our future that you plann'd:
  Only remember me; you understand
It will be late to counsel then or pray.
Yet if you should forget me for a while
  And afterwards remember, do not grieve:
  For if the darkness and corruption leave
A vestige of the thoughts that once I had,
Better by far you should forget and smile
  Than that you should remember and be sad.

❧ Do Not Stand at My Grave and Weep

Mary Elizabeth Frye 1905–2004

Do not stand at my grave and weep,
I am not there; I do not sleep.
I am a thousand winds that blow,
I am the diamond glints on snow,
I am the sun on ripened grain,
I am the gentle autumn rain.
When you awaken in the morning's hush,
I am the swift uplifting rush
Of quiet birds in circling flight.
I am the soft starlight at night.
Do not stand at my grave and cry,
I am not there; I did not die.

❧ Requiem

Robert Louis Stevenson 1850–1894

Under the wide and starry sky,
  Dig the grave and let me lie.
Glad did I live and gladly die,
  And I laid me down with a will.

This be the verse you grave for me:
  Here he lies where he longed to be;
Home is the sailor, home from sea,
  And the hunter home from the hill.

❧ My Funeral

Wendy Cope 1945–

I hope I can trust you, friends, not to use our relationship
As an excuse for an unsolicited ego-trip.
I have seen enough of them at funerals and they make me
    cross.
At this one, though deceased, I aim to be the boss.
If you are asked to talk about me for five minutes, please
    do not go on for eight.
There is a strict timetable at the crematorium and nobody
    wants to be late.
If invited to read a poem, just read the bloody poem.
    If requested
To sing a song, just sing it, as suggested,
And don't say anything. Though I will not be there,
Glancing pointedly at my watch and fixing the speaker
    with a malevolent stare,
Remember that this was how I always reacted
When I felt that anybody's speech, sermon or poetry
    reading was becoming too protracted.
Yes, I was impatient and intolerant, and not always polite
And if there aren't many people at my funeral, it will
    serve me right.

❧ Crossing the Bar

Alfred, Lord Tennyson 1809–1892

Sunset and evening star,
    And one clear call for me!
And may there be no moaning of the bar,
    When I put out to sea,

But such a tide as moving seems asleep,
    Too full for sound and foam,
When that which drew from out the boundless deep
    Turns again home.

Twilight and evening bell,
    And after that the dark!
And may there be no sadness of farewell,
    When I embark;

For tho' from out our bourne of Time and Place
    The flood may bear me far,
I hope to see my Pilot face to face
    When I have crost the bar.

❧ Refusal to Mourn

Andrea Cohen 1961–

In lieu of
flowers, send
him back.

❧ The Day is Done

Henry Wadsworth Longfellow 1807–1882

The day is done, and the darkness
  Falls from the wings of Night,
As a feather is wafted downward
  From an eagle in his flight.

I see the lights of the village
  Gleam through the rain and the mist,
And a feeling of sadness comes o'er me
  That my soul cannot resist:

A feeling of sadness and longing,
  That is not akin to pain,
And resembles sorrow only
  As the mist resembles the rain.

Come, read to me some poem,
  Some simple and heartfelt lay,
That shall soothe this restless feeling,
  And banish the thoughts of day.

Not from the grand old masters,
  Not from the bards sublime,
Whose distant footsteps echo
  Through the corridors of Time.

For, like strains of martial music,
  Their mighty thoughts suggest
Life's endless toil and endeavor;
  And to-night I long for rest.

Read from some humbler poet,
    Whose songs gushed from his heart,
As showers from the clouds of summer,
    Or tears from the eyelids start;

Who, through long days of labor,
    And nights devoid of ease,
Still heard in his soul the music
    Of wonderful melodies.

Such songs have power to quiet
    The restless pulse of care,
And come like the benediction
    That follows after prayer.

Then read from the treasured volume
    The poem of thy choice,
And lend to the rhyme of the poet
    The beauty of thy voice.

And the night shall be filled with music,
    And the cares, that infest the day,
Shall fold their tents, like the Arabs,
    And as silently steal away.

ॐ Scarborough Fair (Folk Song)

Anon

"O, where are you going?" "To Scarborough fair,"
　Savoury sage, rosemary, and thyme;
"Remember me to a lass who lives there,
　For once she was a true love of mine.

"And tell her to make me a cambric shirt,
　Savoury sage, rosemary, and thyme,
Without any seam or needlework,
　And then she shall be a true love of mine.

"And tell her to wash it in yonder dry well,
　Savoury sage, rosemary, and thyme,
Where no water sprung, nor a drop of rain fell,
　And then she shall be a true love of mine.

"And tell her to dry it on yonder thorn,
　Savoury sage, rosemary, and thyme,
Which never bore blossom since Adam was born,
　And then she shall be a true love of thine."

"O, will you find me an acre of land,
　Savoury sage, rosemary, and thyme,
Between the sea foam, the sea sand,
　Or never be a true lover of mine.

"O, will you plough it with a ram's horn,
　Savoury sage, rosemary, and thyme,
And sow it all over with one peppercorn,
　Or never be a true lover of mine.

"O, will you reap it with a sickle of leather,
  Savoury sage, rosemary, and thyme,
And tie it all up with a peacock's feather,
  Or never be a true lover of mine.

"And when you have done and finished your work,
  Savoury sage, rosemary, and thyme,
You may come to me for your cambric shirt,
  And then you shall be a true lover of mine."

❧ Fare You Well (Folk Song)

Anon

Fare you well, my dear, I must be gone,
And leave you for a while;
If I roam away I'll come back again,
Though I roam ten thousand miles, my dear,
Though I roam ten thousand miles.

So fair thou art, my bonny lass,
So deep in love am I;
But I never will prove false to the bonny lass I love,
Till the stars fall from the sky, my dear,
Till the stars fall from the sky.

The sea will never run dry, my dear,
Nor the rocks melt with the sun,
But I never will prove false to the bonny lass I love,
Till all these things be done, my dear,
Till all these things be done.

O yonder doth sit that little turtle dove,
He doth sit on yonder high tree,
A- making a moan for the loss of his love,
As I will do for thee, my dear,
As I will do for thee.

❧ Danny Boy

Frederic Edward Weatherly 1848–1929

Oh, Danny boy, the pipes, the pipes are calling
From glen to glen, and down the mountain side
The summer's gone, and all the flowers are dying
'Tis you, 'tis you must go and I must bide.
But come ye back when summer's in the meadow
Or when the valley's hushed and white with snow
'Tis I'll be here in sunshine or in shadow
Oh Danny boy, oh Danny boy, I love you so.

And when you come, and all the flowers are dying
If I am dead, as dead I well may be
You'll come and find the place where I am lying
And kneel and say an "Ave" there for me.
And I shall hear, tho' soft you tread above me
And all my dreams will warm and sweeter be
If you'll not fail to tell me that you love me
I'll simply sleep in peace until you come to me.
I'll simply sleep in peace until you come to me.

🐦 Molly Malone (Folk Song)

Anon

In Dublin's fair city where the girls are so pretty
'Twas there that I first met sweet Molly Malone
She wheeled her wheelbarrow thru the streets broad and
  narrow
Crying "cockles and mussels alive alive-o!"
Alive alive-o, alive alive-o!
Crying "cockles and mussels alive alive o!"

She was a fishmonger but sure 'twas no wonder
For so were her father and mother before
And they each wheel'd their barrow thru the streets broad
  and narrow
Crying "cockles and mussels alive alive o!"
Alive alive-o, alive alive-o!
Crying "cockles and mussels alive alive o!"

She died of a fever and no one could save her
And that was the end of sweet Molly Malone
Her ghost wheels her barrow thru the streets broad and
  narrow
Crying "cockles and mussels alive alive-o!"
Alive alive-o, alive alive-o!
Crying "cockles and mussels alive alive o!"

❧ O Captain, My Captain

Walt Whitman 1819–1892

O Captain! my Captain! our fearful trip is done,
The ship has weather'd every rack, the prize we sought is
    won,
The port is near, the bells I hear, the people all exulting,
While follow eyes the steady keel, the vessel grim and
    daring;
        But O heart! heart! heart!
         O the bleeding drops of red,
           Where on the deck my Captain lies,
          Fallen cold and dead.

O Captain! my Captain! rise up and hear the bells;
Rise up—for you the flag is flung—for you the bugle
    trills,
For you bouquets and ribbon'd wreaths—for you the
    shores a-crowding,
For you they call, the swaying mass, their eager faces
    turning;
        Here Captain! dear father!
        This arm beneath your head!
          It is some dream that on the deck,
         You've fallen cold and dead.

My Captain does not answer, his lips are pale and still,
My father does not feel my arm, he has no pulse nor will,
The ship is anchor'd safe and sound, its voyage closed and
  done,
From fearful trip the victor ship comes in with object won;
        Exult O shores, and ring O bells!
          But I with mournful tread,
            Walk the deck my Captain lies,
              Fallen cold and dead.

❧ How Clear, How Lovely Bright

A.E. Housman 1859–1936

How clear, how lovely bright,
How beautiful to sight
　　Those beams of morning play;
How heaven laughs out with glee
Where, like a bird set free,
Up from the eastern sea
　　Soars the delightful day.

To-day I shall be strong,
No more shall yield to wrong,
　　Shall squander life no more;
Days lost, I know not how,
I shall retrieve them now;
Now I shall keep the vow
　　I never kept before.

Ensanguining the skies
How heavily it dies
　　Into the west away;
Past touch and sight and sound
Not further to be found,
How hopeless under ground
　　Falls the remorseful day.

❧ Healings 2

Kathleen Jamie 1962–

At midnight the north sky is blues and greys,
with a thin fissure of citrine just above the
horizon. It's light when you wake, regardless of
the hour. At 2 or 4 or 6am, you breathe light
into your body.
A rose, a briar rose. A wild rose and its thorned
stem. What did Burns say? 'you seize the flo'er,
the bloom is shed'.
To be healed is not to be saved from mortality,
but rather, released back into it: we are
returned to the wild, into possibilities for
ageing and change.

December

Celebrations

WITH the year's longest nights, it is perhaps unsurprising that December has always been a month for celebrations and revelry. In ancient Greece, the midwinter festival of Dionysia celebrated Dionysus, the god of partying and wine, with an emphasis on drinking and theatrical performances – the ancestor of today's pantomime season. In Britain, the Pagan feast of Yule long predated Christmas, before eventually being subsumed into it. As in Thomas Campion's poem, it seems a relatively natural transition from 'Now winter nights enlarge / The number of their hours' to 'Let now the chimneys blaze / And cups o'erflow with wine'. From W.B. Yeats' pithy drinking song via Ogden Nash's comic epigram to a toast by the ancient Chinese poet Du Fu, here bacchanal verse abounds.

But entertainment is only one aspect of celebration. As the year draws to a close, December is a time to celebrate the old year and the new year, each other and ourselves. Acknowledging oneself is a subject the poets turn to: as the cult hero Charles Bukowski writes, 'you are marvelous / the gods wait/ to delight in you.' Maya Angelou's iconic Black feminist anthem crowns a run of poems about self-celebration, with the likes of Nikita Gill and Phoebe Stuckes taking up the mantle of Angelou's legacy in the younger British poetry movement.

Love also comes in for attention in these celebratory poems. Amy Levy, a contemporary of Oscar Wilde, lived the whole of her brief life on the margins. She was only the second Jewish woman to study at Cambridge and was known to have romantic affairs with both women and men at a time when it was far from being socially accepted. But her poem here is enhanced by that peripherality, celebrating the thrill of a secret love. Frank O'Hara, one of the leaders of the New York School of Poets of the 1950s and 60s, follows here with a breathlessly ecstatic piece celebrating a love from a time 'when we were still first rate'. Likely addressing his muse and lover, Vincent Warren, O'Hara's nostalgia accelerates until he reaches the present tense: 'I wouldn't want to be faster / or greener than now if you were with me O you / were the best of all my days.'

And yet sometimes a celebration needs no specific object; we might bask in the beauty of nature or the symphony of natural sounds. Poets are endlessly inspired by birdsong, as the poems throughout this year have shown; it is the birds' unique ability to freely warble on, gloriously revelling in nothing in particular. Thomas Hardy's 'The Darkling Thrush', shows how the 'ecstatic sound' of a 'frail, gaunt, and small' thrush's 'full-hearted evensong' is enough to transform the bleak wintry evening into a rejoicing moment. Other poets seize on something similar. For Oliver Herford, birdsong is 'magical', like his verse: 'We are nearer to Spring / Than we were in September,' / I heard a bird sing / In the dark of December.' It is so easy to feel that the winter will never end – but the 'dark of December' is a promise that the worst of the year is over and that spring will soon come.

The poems included for the festive season are, above all, varied. There are of course the classics, evoking childhood memories with their first lines alone. The excitement stirred up by Clement Clarke Moore's opening lines – ''Twas the night before Christmas, when all through the house / Not a creature was stirring, not even a mouse' – is only heightened by delivering it in the customary whisper; and who can read Christina Rossetti's classic 'In the bleak midwinter . . .' without singing the hymn silently, inside their head? But these sit alongside Wendy

Cope's brilliantly unsentimental take on the festive season and Emily Dickinson's experimental work. It is Dickinson's vague, and yet assured, promise of 'wonder upon wonder' that encapsulates the mood for this month's poems best.

And finally, of course, we come to celebrating the end of the year. Throughout human history – and still to this day – the Gregorian calendar is just one among many ways of measuring the year – but no matter when a year is considered to begin and end, it has always been a cause for celebration. Whether celebrated by fireworks or religious festivities, a new year has always been seen as an opportunity to set new goals and make new plans, to look forward with optimism and hope. And while no series of New Year's Eve poems could be complete without Robert Burns, the quintessential bard of Scotland, the monumental 'Auld Lang Syne' is far from the only New Year's anthem collected here. It sits alongside D.H. Lawrence's risqué midnight tercets, an electrifying 1995 poem by Naomi Shihab Nye, and a jubilant extract from Tennyson's 'In Memoriam', which finally sums everything up: 'Ring, happy bells, across the snow:/ The year is going, let him go'.

Just like moons and like suns,
With the certainty of tides,
Just like hopes springing high,
Still I'll rise.

Maya Angelou

❧ A Drinking Song

W.B. Yeats 1865–1939

Wine comes in at the mouth
And love comes in at the eye;
That's all we shall know for truth
Before we grow old and die.
I lift the glass to my mouth,
I look at you, and I sigh.

❧ Reflections On Ice Breaking

Ogden Nash 1902–1971

Candy
Is dandy
But liquor
Is quicker.

❧ A Toast for Men Yun-Ch'ing

Du Fu 712 AD–770 AD
Translated by Florence Ayscough

Illimitable happiness,
But grief for our white heads.
We love the long watches of the night, the red candle.
It would be difficult to have too much of meeting,
Let us not be in hurry to talk of separation.
But because the Heaven River will sink,
We had better empty the wine-cups.
To-morrow, at bright dawn, the world's business will
    entangle us.
We brush away our tears,
We go—East and West.

🪶 The Wine of Love

James Thomson 1700–1748

The wine of Love is music,
    And the feast of Love is song:
And when Love sits down to the banquet,
    Love sits long:

Sits long and ariseth drunken,
    But not with the feast and the wine;
He reeleth with his own heart,
    That great rich Vine.

❧ First Fig

Edna St. Vincent Millay 1892–1950

My candle burns at both ends;
   It will not last the night;
But ah, my foes, and oh, my friends—
   It gives a lovely light!

❧ The Laughing Heart

Charles Bukowski 1920–1994

your life is your life
don't let it be clubbed into dank submission.
be on the watch.
there are ways out.
there is a light somewhere.
it may not be much light but
it beats the darkness.
be on the watch.
the gods will offer you chances.
know them.
take them.
you can't beat death but
you can beat death in life, sometimes.
and the more often you learn to do it,
the more light there will be.
your life is your life.
know it while you have it.
you are marvelous
the gods wait to delight
in you.

❧ Still I Rise

Maya Angelou 1928–2014

You may write me down in history
With your bitter, twisted lies,
You may trod me in the very dirt
But still, like dust, I'll rise.

Does my sassiness upset you?
Why are you beset with gloom?
'Cause I walk like I've got oil wells
Pumping in my living room.
Just like moons and like suns,
With the certainty of tides,
Just like hopes springing high,
Still I'll rise.

Did you want to see me broken?
Bowed head and lowered eyes?
Shoulders falling down like teardrops,
Weakened by my soulful cries?

Does my haughtiness offend you?
Don't you take it awful hard
'Cause I laugh like I've got gold mines
Diggin' in my own backyard.

You may shoot me with your words,
You may cut me with your eyes,
You may kill me with your hatefulness,
But still, like air, I'll rise.

Does my sexiness upset you?
Does it come as a surprise
That I dance like I've got diamonds
At the meeting of my thighs?

Out of the huts of history's shame
I rise
Up from a past that's rooted in pain
I rise
I'm a black ocean, leaping and wide,
Welling and swelling I bear in the tide.

Leaving behind nights of terror and fear
I rise
Into a daybreak that's wondrously clear
I rise
Bringing the gifts that my ancestors gave,
I am the dream and the hope of the slave.
I rise
I rise
I rise.

❧ Daughters

Phoebe Stuckes 1996–

Enough of pulling off high heels to run
Or else waiting alone in unclaimed ugliness.

No more crying out for guitar heroes
Or going back to old loves for the safety.

Let us build bonfires of those unanswered prayers.
Let us learn how to leave with clean and empty hearts
Let us escape these attics still mad, still drunk, still raving
Let us vacate these badly lit odd little towns
Let us want none of what anchored our mothers
Let us never evolve to be good or beautiful
Let us spit and snarl and rattle the hatches
Let us never be conquered
Let us no longer keep keys in our knuckles
Let us run into the streets hungry, fervent, ablaze.

You
Are a mighty thing
A captive animal, woken with a taste for blood.
Feed it,

You Amazon, you Gloria, you Swiss army knife of a
    woman.

ॐ Tell your Daughters

Nikita Gill 1987–

Tell your daughters how you love your body.
Tell them how they must love theirs.

Tell them to be proud of every bit of themselves –
from their tiger stripes to the soft flesh of their thighs,
whether there is a little of them or a lot,
whether freckles cover their face or not,
whether their curves are plentiful or slim,
whether their hair is thick, curly, straight, long or short.

Tell them how they inherited
their ancestors' souls in their smiles,
that their eyes carry countries
that breathed life into history,
that the swing of their hips
does not determine their destiny.

Tell them never to listen when bodies are critiqued.
Tell them every woman's body is beautiful
because every woman's soul is unique.

🐦 Someday I'll love Ocean Vuong

Ocean Vuong 1988–

Ocean, don't be afraid.
The end of the road is so far ahead
it is already behind us.
Don't worry. Your father is only your father
until one of you forgets. Like how the spine
won't remember its wings
no matter how many times our knees
kiss the pavement. Ocean,
are you listening? The most beautiful part
of your body is wherever
your mother's shadow falls.
Here's the house with childhood
whittled down to a single red tripwire.
Don't worry. Just call it *horizon*
& you'll never reach it.
Here's today. Jump. I promise it's not
a lifeboat. Here's the man
whose arms are wide enough to gather
your leaving. & here the moment,
just after the lights go out, when you can still see
the faint torch between his legs.
How you use it again & again
to find your own hands.
You asked for a second chance
& are given a mouth to empty into.
Don't be afraid, the gunfire
is only the sound of people
trying to live a little longer. Ocean. Ocean,
get up. The most beautiful part of your body

is where it's headed. & remember,
loneliness is still time spent
with the world. Here's
the room with everyone in it.
Your dead friends passing
through you like wind
through a wind chime. Here's a desk
with the gimp leg & a brick
to make it last. Yes, here's a room
so warm & blood-close,
I swear, you will wake—
& mistake these walls
for skin.

❧ Cabin Baggage

Clive James 1939-2019

My niece is heading here to stay with us.
Before she leaves home she takes careful stock
Of what she might not know again for years.
The berries (so she writes) have been brought in,
But she'll be gone before the peaches come.
On days of burning sun, the air is tinged
With salt and eucalyptus. 'Why am I
Leaving all this behind? I feel a fool.'
But I can tell from how she writes things down
The distance will assist her memories
To take full form. She travels to stay still.
I wish I'd been that smart before I left.
Instead, I have to dig deep for a trace
Of how the beach was red hot underfoot,
The green gold of the Christmas beetle's wing.

❧ Hymn to Time

Ursula K. Le Guin 1929–2018

Time says "Let there be"
every moment and instantly
there is space and the radiance
of each bright galaxy.

And eyes beholding radiance.
And the gnats' flickering dance.
And the seas' expanse.
And death, and chance.

Time makes room
for going and coming home
and in time's womb
begins all ending.

Time is being and being
time, it is all one thing,
the shining, the seeing,
the dark abounding.

❧ At a Dinner Party

Amy Levy 1861–1889

With fruit and flowers the board is decked,
　The wine and laughter flow;
I'll not complain—could one expect
　So dull a world to know?

You look across the fruit and flowers,
　My glance your glances find.—
It is our secret, only ours,
　Since all the world is blind.

❧ Animals

Frank O'Hara 1926–1966

Have you forgotten what we were like then
when we were still first rate
and the day came fat with an apple in its mouth

it's no use worrying about Time
but we did have a few tricks up our sleeves
and turned some sharp corners

the whole pasture looked like our meal
we didn't need speedometers
we could manage cocktails out of ice and water

I wouldn't want to be faster
or greener than now if you were with me O you
were the best of all my days

❧ Now Winter Nights Enlarge

Thomas Campion 1567–1620

Now winter nights enlarge
The number of their hours;
And clouds their storms discharge
Upon the airy towers.
Let now the chimneys blaze
And cups o'erflow with wine,
Let well-turned words amaze
With harmony divine.
Now yellow waxen lights
Shall wait on honey love
While youthful revels, masques, and courtly sights
Sleep's leaden spells remove.

This time doth well dispense
With lovers' long discourse;
Much speech hath some defense,
Though beauty no remorse.
All do not all things well;
Some measures comely tread,
Some knotted riddles tell,
Some poems smoothly read.
The summer hath his joys,
And winter his delights;
Though love and all his pleasures are but toys,
They shorten tedious nights.

❧ Winter-Time

Robert Louis Stevenson 1850–1894

Late lies the wintry sun a-bed,
A frosty, fiery sleepy-head;
Blinks but an hour or two; and then,
A blood-red orange, sets again.

Before the stars have left the skies,
At morning in the dark I rise;
And shivering in my nakedness,
By the cold candle, bathe and dress.

Close by the jolly fire I sit
To warm my frozen bones a bit;
Or with a reindeer-sled, explore
The colder countries round the door.

When to go out, my nurse doth wrap
Me in my comforter and cap;
The cold wind burns my face, and blows
Its frosty pepper up my nose.

Black are my steps on silver sod;
Thick blows my frosty breath abroad;
And tree and house, and hill and lake,
Are frosted like a wedding-cake.

❧ I Heard a Bird Sing

Oliver Herford 1860–1935

I heard a bird sing
In the dark of December.
A magical thing
And sweet to remember.

"We are nearer to Spring
Than we were in September,"
I heard a bird sing
In the dark of December.

❧ Pied Beauty

Gerard Manley Hopkins 1844–1889

Glory be to God for dappled things –
　　For skies of couple-colour as a brinded cow;
　　　　For rose-moles all in stipple upon trout that swim;
Fresh-firecoal chestnut-falls; finches' wings;
　　Landscape plotted and pieced – fold, fallow, and plough;
　　　　And áll trádes, their gear and tackle and trim.

All things counter, original, spare, strange;
　　Whatever is fickle, freckled (who knows how?)
　　　　With swift, slow; sweet, sour; adazzle, dim;
He fathers-forth whose beauty is past change:
　　　　　　Praise him.

?❧ The Darkling Thrush

Thomas Hardy 1840–1928

I leant upon a coppice gate
　When Frost was spectre-gray,
And Winter's dregs made desolate
　The weakening eye of day.
The tangled bine-stems scored the sky
　Like strings of broken lyres,
And all mankind that haunted nigh
　Had sought their household fires.

The land's sharp features seemed to be
　The Century's corpse outleant,
His crypt the cloudy canopy,
　The wind his death-lament.
The ancient pulse of germ and birth
　Was shrunken hard and dry,
And every spirit upon earth
　Seemed fervourless as I.

At once a voice arose among
　The bleak twigs overhead
In a full-hearted evensong
　Of joy illimited;
An aged thrush, frail, gaunt, and small,
　In blast-beruffled plume,
Had chosen thus to fling his soul
　Upon the growing gloom.

So little cause for carolings
   Of such ecstatic sound
Was written on terrestrial things
   Afar or nigh around,
That I could think there trembled through
   His happy good-night air
Some blessed Hope, whereof he knew
   And I was unaware.

❧ A Christmas Poem

Wendy Cope 1945–

At Christmas little children sing and merry bells jingle,
The cold winter air makes our hands and faces tingle
And happy families go to church and cheerily they mingle
And the whole business is unbelievably dreadful, if you're
single.

❧ Before the ice is in the pools

Emily Dickinson 1830–1886

Before the ice is in the pools –
Before the skaters go,
Or any check at nightfall
Is tarnished by the snow –

Before the fields have finished –
Before the Christmas tree,
Wonder upon wonder –
Will arrive to me!

What we touch the hems of
On a summer's day –
What is only walking
Just a bridge away –

That which sings so – speaks so –
When there's no one here –
Will the frock I wept in
Answer me to wear?

❧ In the Bleak Midwinter

Christina Rossetti 1830–1894

In the bleak midwinter, frosty wind made moan,
Earth stood hard as iron, water like a stone;
Snow had fallen, snow on snow, snow on snow,
In the bleak midwinter, long ago.

Our God, Heaven cannot hold Him, nor earth sustain;
Heaven and earth shall flee away when He comes to reign.
In the bleak midwinter a stable place sufficed
The Lord God Almighty, Jesus Christ.

Enough for Him, whom cherubim, worship night and day,
Breastful of milk, and a mangerful of hay;
Enough for Him, whom angels fall before,
The ox and ass and camel which adore.

Angels and archangels may have gathered there,
Cherubim and seraphim thronged the air;
But His mother only, in her maiden bliss,
Worshipped the beloved with a kiss.

What can I give Him, poor as I am?
If I were a shepherd, I would bring a lamb;
If I were a Wise Man, I would do my part;
Yet what I can I give Him: give my heart.

❧ I Saw a Stable

Mary Elizabeth Coleridge 1861–1907

I saw a stable, low and very bare,
A little child in a manger.
The oxen knew Him, had Him in their care,
To men He was a stranger.
The safety of the world was lying there,
And the world's danger.

🐦 A Visit from St. Nicholas

Clement Clarke Moore 1779–1863

'Twas the night before Christmas, when all through the
  house
Not a creature was stirring, not even a mouse;
The stockings were hung by the chimney with care,
In hopes that St. Nicholas soon would be there;
The children were nestled all snug in their beds;
While visions of sugar-plums danced in their heads;
And mamma in her 'kerchief, and I in my cap,
Had just settled our brains for a long winter's nap,
When out on the lawn there arose such a clatter,
I sprang from my bed to see what was the matter.
Away to the window I flew like a flash,
Tore open the shutters and threw up the sash.
The moon on the breast of the new-fallen snow,
Gave a lustre of midday to objects below,
When what to my wondering eyes did appear,
But a miniature sleigh and eight tiny rein-deer,
With a little old driver so lively and quick,
I knew in a moment he must be St. Nick.
More rapid than eagles his coursers they came,
And he whistled, and shouted, and called them by name:
"Now, *Dasher*! now, *Dancer*! now *Prancer* and *Vixen*!
On, *Comet*! on, *Cupid*! on, *Donner* and *Blitzen*!
To the top of the porch! to the top of the wall!
Now dash away! dash away! dash away all!"
As leaves that before the wild hurricane fly,
When they meet with an obstacle, mount to the sky;
So up to the housetop the coursers they flew
With the sleigh full of toys, and St. Nicholas too—

And then, in a twinkling, I heard on the roof
The prancing and pawing of each little hoof.
As I drew in my head, and was turning around,
Down the chimney St. Nicholas came with a bound.
He was dressed all in fur, from his head to his foot,
And his clothes were all tarnished with ashes and soot;
A bundle of toys he had flung on his back,
And he looked like a pedler just opening his pack.
His eyes—how they twinkled! his dimples, how merry!
His cheeks were like roses, his nose like a cherry!
His droll little mouth was drawn up like a bow,
And the beard on his chin was as white as the snow;
The stump of a pipe he held tight in his teeth,
And the smoke, it encircled his head like a wreath;
He had a broad face and a little round belly
That shook when he laughed, like a bowl full of jelly.
He was chubby and plump, a right jolly old elf,
And I laughed when I saw him, in spite of myself;
A wink of his eye and a twist of his head
Soon gave me to know I had nothing to dread;
He spoke not a word, but went straight to his work,
And filled all the stockings; then turned with a jerk,
And laying his finger aside of his nose,
And giving a nod, up the chimney he rose;
He sprang to his sleigh, to his team gave a whistle,
And away they all flew like the down of a thistle.
But I heard him exclaim, ere he drove out of sight—
"Happy Christmas to all, and to all a good night!"

❧ The Oxen

Thomas Hardy 1840–1928

Christmas Eve, and twelve of the clock.
"Now they are all on their knees,"
An elder said as we sat in a flock
By the embers in hearthside ease.

We pictured the meek mild creatures where
They dwelt in their strawy pen,
Nor did it occur to one of us there
To doubt they were kneeling then.

So fair a fancy few would weave
In these years! Yet, I feel,
If someone said on Christmas Eve,
"Come; see the oxen kneel,

"In the lonely barton by yonder coomb
Our childhood used to know,"
I should go with him in the gloom,
Hoping it might be so.

❧ Burning the Old Year

Naomi Shihab Nye 1952–

Letters swallow themselves in seconds.
Notes friends tied to the doorknob,
transparent scarlet paper,
sizzle like moth wings,
marry the air.

So much of any year is flammable,
lists of vegetables, partial poems.
Orange swirling flame of days,
so little is a stone.

Where there was something and suddenly isn't,
an absence shouts, celebrates, leaves a space.
I begin again with the smallest numbers.

Quick dance, shuffle of losses and leaves,
only the things I didn't do
crackle after the blazing dies.

❧ From *The Tempest* (Act 4, Scene 1)

William Shakespeare 1564–1616

Our revels now are ended. These our actors,
As I foretold you, were all spirits, and
Are melted into air, into thin air;
And, like the baseless fabric of this vision,
The cloud-capped towers, the gorgeous palaces,
The solemn temples, the great globe itself,
Yea, all which it inherit, shall dissolve,
And, like this insubstantial pageant faded,
Leave not a rack behind. We are such stuff
As dreams are made on, and our little life
Is rounded with a sleep.

❧ The Old Year

John Clare 1793–1864

The Old Year's gone away
   To nothingness and night:
We cannot find him all the day
   Nor hear him in the night:
He left no footstep, mark or place
   In either shade or sun:
The last year he'd a neighbour's face,
   In this he's known by none.

All nothing everywhere:
   Mists we on mornings see
Have more of substance when they're here
   And more of form than he.
He was a friend by every fire,
   In every cot and hall—
A guest to every heart's desire,
   And now he's nought at all.

Old papers thrown away,
   Old garments cast aside,
The talk of yesterday,
   Are things identified;
But time once torn away
   No voices can recall:
The eve of New Year's Day
   Left the Old Year lost to all.

❧ Auld Lang Syne

Robert Burns 1759–1796

Should auld acquaintance be forgot,
And never brought to mind?
Should auld acquaintance be forgot,
And auld lang syne!

For auld lang syne, my dear,
For auld lang syne.
We'll tak a cup o' kindness yet,
For auld lang syne.

And surely ye'll be your pint stowp!
And surely I'll be mine!
And we'll tak a cup o' kindness yet,
For auld lang syne.

For auld lang syne, my dear,
For auld lang syne.
We'll tak a cup o' kindness yet,
For auld lang syne.

We twa hae run about the braes,
And pou'd the gowans fine;
But we've wander'd mony a weary fit,
Sin' auld lang syne.

For auld lang syne, my dear,
For auld lang syne.
We'll tak a cup o' kindness yet,
For auld lang syne.

We twa hae paidl'd in the burn,
Frae morning sun till dine;
But seas between us braid hae roar'd
Sin' auld lang syne.

For auld lang syne, my dear,
For auld lang syne.
We'll tak a cup o' kindness yet,
For auld lang syne.

And there's a hand, my trusty fere!
And gie's a hand o' thine!
And we'll tak a right gude-willie waught,
For auld lang syne.

For auld lang syne, my dear,
For auld lang syne.
We'll tak a cup o' kindness yet,
For auld lang syne.

❧ New Year's Eve

D.H. Lawrence 1885–1930

There are only two things now,
The great black night scooped out
And this fireglow.

This fireglow, the core,
And we the two ripe pips
That are held in store.

Listen, the darkness rings
As it circulates round our fire.
Take off your things.

Your shoulders, your bruised throat!
You breasts, your nakedness!
This fiery coat!

As the darkness flickers and dips,
As the firelight falls and leaps
From your feet to your lips!

❧ Ring out, wild bells (*from* In Memoriam)

Alfred, Lord Tennyson 1809–1892

Ring out, wild bells, to the wild sky,
    The flying cloud, the frosty light:
    The year is dying in the night;
Ring out, wild bells, and let him die.

Ring out the old, ring in the new,
    Ring, happy bells, across the snow:
    The year is going, let him go;
Ring out the false, ring in the true.

Ring out the grief that saps the mind
    For those that here we see no more;
    Ring out the feud of rich and poor,
Ring in redress to all mankind.

Ring out a slowly dying cause,
    And ancient forms of party strife;
    Ring in the nobler modes of life,
With sweeter manners, purer laws.

Ring out the want, the care, the sin,
    The faithless coldness of the times;
    Ring out, ring out my mournful rhymes
But ring the fuller minstrel in.

Ring out false pride in place and blood,
　The civic slander and the spite;
　Ring in the love of truth and right,
Ring in the common love of good.

Ring out old shapes of foul disease;
　Ring out the narrowing lust of gold;
　Ring out the thousand wars of old,
Ring in the thousand years of peace.

Ring in the valiant man and free,
　The larger heart, the kindlier hand;
　Ring out the darkness of the land,
Ring in the Christ that is to be.

Index of First Lines

Index of Poets and Translators

Acknowledgements

With thanks to everyone at Bluebird and to Jaime Witcomb, Stevie Doran and Scarlet Katz Roberts.

The compiler and publisher would like to thank the following for permission to use copyright material:

Adcock, Fleur 'Coupling' from *Collected Poems* (Bloodaxe Books, 2024). Reprinted with permission of Bloodaxe Books. **Addonizio, Kim** 'To the Woman Crying Uncontrollably in the Next Stall'. Reprinted with permission of the author. **Angelou, Maya** 'Phenomenal Woman' and 'Still I Rise' from *And Still I Rise* (Little Brown). Reproduced with permission of Little Brown through PLSclear. **Antrobus, Raymond** 'And That' from *All the Names Given* by Raymond Antrobus © Raymond Antrobus, 2021, published by Picador, reproduced by kind permission by David Higham Associates. 'Happy Birthday Moon' from *The Perseverance*, Penned in the Margins, 2018. **Armitage, Simon** 'Let Me Put it This Way' from *Book of Matches*. Reprinted by permission of Faber and Faber Ltd. **Auden, W.H.** 'FUNERAL BLUES' Copyright © 1940 by W.H. Auden, renewed. Reprinted by permission of Curtis Brown, Ltd. All rights reserved. 'O Tell Me the Truth About Love' Copyright © 1940 by W.H. Auden, renewed. Reprinted by permission of Curtis Brown, Ltd. All rights reserved. 'If I Could Tell You' Copyright © 1945 by W.H. Auden, renewed. Reprinted by permission of Curtis Brown, Ltd. All rights reserved. **Barks, Coleman** 'The Guest House' from *Selected Poems by Rumi* published by Penguin Classics. Translation Copyright © Coleman Barks, 1995. Reprinted by permission of Penguin Books Limited. **Berry, Wendell** 'The Peace of Wild Things' from *New Collected Poems*. Copyright © 2012 by Wendell Berry. Reprinted with the permission of The Permissions Company, LLC on behalf of Counterpoint Press, counterpointpress.com. **Bilston, Brian** 'A Brief History of Modern Art in Poetry' from *Diary of a Somebody*. 'Serenity Prayer' from *Alexa, what is there to know about love?* Reprinted by

of the Estate of C. Day-Lewis. **Dharker, Imtiaz** 'Minority' from *Postcards from god* (Bloodaxe Books, 1997). Reprinted with permission of Bloodaxe Books. **Donaghy, Michael** 'The Present' from *Collected Poems* (2009) reprinted by permission of Picador. **Duffy, Carol Ann** 'Prayer' from *New Selected Poems* by Carol Ann Duffy. Published by Picador, 2004. Copyright © Carol Ann Duffy. Reproduced by permission of the author c/o Rogers, Coleridge & White Ltd., 20 Powis Mews, London W11 1JN. 'Words, Wide Night' from *The Other Country* by Carol Ann Duffy. Published by Anvil Press Poetry, 1990. Copyright © Carol Ann Duffy. Reproduced by permission of the author c/o Rogers, Coleridge & White Ltd., 20 Powis Mews, London W11 1JN 'Empty Nest' from *Empty Nest* by Carol Ann Duffy. Published by Picador, 2021. Copyright © Carol Ann Duffy. Reproduced by permission of the author c/o Rogers, Coleridge & White Ltd., 20 Powis Mews, London W11 1JN. **Dunmore, Helen** 'Hold out your arms' from *Counting Backwards: Poems 1975-2017* (Bloodaxe Books, 2019). Reprinted with permission of Bloodaxe Books. **Duhig, Ian** 'Bridled Vows' from *The Blind Roadmaker*. Reproduced by permission of Picador. **Eliot, T.S.** 'Little Gidding' taken from *Four Quartets*. Reprinted by permission of Faber and Faber Ltd. **Fanthorpe, U.A.** 'Atlas' from *Selected Poems* (Enitharmon Press, 2013). **Fenton, James** 'Hinterhof' from *Yellow Tulips*. Reprinted by permission of Faber and Faber Ltd. **Fishback, Margaret** 'Virtue is its Own Reward' from *I Feel Better Now*. Copyright © 1932 by Margaret Fishback. Reprinted by permission of Anthony Antolini. 'Into Each Life Some Rain Must Fall' from *Out of My Head* (E. P. Dutton, 1933). Reprinted by permission of Anthony Antolini. **Flynn, Leontia** 'The Furthest Distances I've Travelled' from *These Days* by Leontia Flynn published by Jonathan Cape. Copyright © Leontia Flynn, 2004. Reprinted by permission of The Random House Group Limited. **Gaiman, Neil** 'Dark Sonnets' copyright © 2005 by Neil Gaiman. Reprinted by permission of Writers House LLC acting as agent for the author. 'Wedding Thoughts: All I Know About Love' copyright © 2017 by Neil Gaiman. Reprinted by permission of Writers House LLC acting as agent for the author. **Gill, Nikita** 'Tell Your Daughters' from The Girl and the Goddess by Nikita Gill published by Ebury Press. Copyright © Nikita Gill, 2020. Reprinted by permission of The Random House Group Limited. **Gillingham, Erica** 'Let's Make a Baby with Science' was first published in *Untitled: Voices 1:1*. **Godden, Salena** 'Courage is a Muscle' Reprinted by permission of OWN IT! **Graves, Robert** 'Love at First Sight' from *Complete Poems Vol I (1995)*. Reprinted by permission of Carcanet Press Ltd. **Gray, Ann** 'Love Listen' Reprinted with permission of the author. **Harjo, Joy** 'For Keeps', from *CONFLICT RESOLUTION FOR HOLY BEINGS: POEMS* by Joy Harjo. Copyright © 2015 by Joy Harjo. 'Remember'. Copyright © 1983 by Joy Harjo, from *SHE HAD SOME HORSES* by Joy Harjo. Used by permission of W. W. Norton & Company, Inc. **Harrison, Tony** 'Long Distance II' taken from *Collected Poems by Tony Harrison* © Tony Harrison and reprinted by permission of Faber and Faber Ltd. **Hass, Robert** 'Half Asleep', 'Mosquito' and 'The Old Pond' from *The Essential Haiku: Versions of Basho, Buson and Issa* (Ecco, 2013; Bloodaxe Books, 2013). Reproduced by permission of Bloodaxe Books. **Heaney, Seamus** 'Blackberry Picking' and 'Scaffolding' from *100 Poems: Seamus Heaney*. Reprinted by permission of Faber and Faber Ltd.

with permission of Lewinsohn Literary Ltd. **Merwin, W.S.** 'Separation' from *Selected Poems* (Bloodaxe Books, 2007). Reprinted with permission of Bloodaxe Books. **Milne, A.A.** 'Us Two' from *Now We Are Six* by A.A. Milne Copyright © Pooh Properties Trust 1924 Reproduced with permissions from Curtis Brown Group Ltd on behalf of The Pooh Properties Trust. **Miłosz, Czesław** 'Gift' from *New and Collected Poems 1931-2001* by Czesław Miłosz published by Penguin Classics. Copyright © Czesław Miłosz Royalties Inc. 1988, 1991, 1995, 2001. Reprinted by permission of Penguin Books Limited. **Mitchell, Adrian** 'Celia, Celia'. Reprinted by permission of United Agents. **Nagra, Daljit** 'Look there goes my father, even now' from *Tippoo Sultan's Incredible White-Man-Eating Tiger Toy-Machine!!!* Reprinted by permission of Faber and Faber Ltd. **Nash, Ogden** 'Reflections on Ice Breaking' from *Candy Is Dandy* (1994) Reprinted by permission of Welbeck Publishing Group (Formerly Carlton Books Ltd). **Nye, Naomi Shihab** 'Fuel' from *Fuel: Poems*. Copyright © 1998 by Naomi Shihab Nye. Reprinted with the permission of The Permissions Company, LLC on behalf of BOA Editions, Ltd., boaeditions.org. 'Burning the old year' and 'Kindness' By permission of the author, Naomi Shihab Nye, 2023. **O'Donoghue, Bernard** 'Going without Saying from *Gunpowder* (Chatto, 1995), reproduced by permission of the author.' **O'Donohue, John** Excerpt from 'For the Break-Up of a Relationship' from *Benedictus* by John O'Donohue published by Bantam Press. Copyright © John O'Donohue, 2007. Reprinted by permission of The Random House Group Limited. **O'Hara, Frank** 'Having a Coke with You,' and 'Animals' from *THE COLLECTED POEMS OF FRANK O'HARA* by Frank O'Hara, copyright © 1971 by Maureen Granville-Smith, Administratrix of the Estate of Frank O'Hara, copyright renewed 1999 by Maureen O'Hara Granville-Smith and Donald Allen. Used by permission of Alfred A. Knopf, an imprint of the Knopf Doubleday Publishing Group, a division of Penguin Random House LLC. All rights reserved. **Osborne, John** 'There Is Handholding Still' reprinted by permission of the author. **Oliver, Mary** 'I Worried' by Mary Oliver. Reprinted by the permission of The Charlotte Sheedy Literary Agency as agent for the author. Copyright © 2010, 2017 by Mary Oliver with permission of Bill Reichblum. 'Wild Geese' from *Dream Work*. Reprinted by the permission of Grove Atlantic. **Oswald, Alice** 'Wedding' from *Thing In the Gap Stone Stile*. Reprinted by permission of Faber and Faber Ltd. **Padgett, Ron** 'Words from the Front' is used by permission from *How to Be Perfect* (Coffee House Press, 2008). Copyright © 2008 by Ron Padgett. **Paterson, Don** 'Rain' from *Rain* by Don Paterson. Published by Faber & Faber Ltd., 2009. Copyright © Don Paterson. Reproduced by permission of the author c/o Rogers, Coleridge & White Ltd., 20 Powis Mews, London W11 1JN. **Piercy, Marge** 'The Birthday of the World' reprinted by permission of Robin Straus Agency. **Plath, Sylvia** 'Morning Song' from *Collected Poems by Sylvia Plath*. Reprinted by permission of Faber and Faber Ltd. **Pugh, Sheenagh** 'What If This Road' by Sheenagh Pugh, from *Id's Hospit* (Seren, 1997). **Roberts, Michael Symmons** 'The Vows' from *Selected Poems* by Michael Symmons Roberts published by Jonathan Cape. Copyright © Michael Symmons Roberts, 2016. Reprinted by permission of The Random House Group Limited. **Robinson, Roger** 'Grace' from *A Portable Paradise* (Peepal Tree Press, 2019) © Roger Robinson, reproduced by permission of Peepal Tree Press. **Sexton, Anne** 'The Fury